Inheriting Our Mothers' Gardens

Inheriting Our Mothers' Gardens

Feminist Theology in Third World Perspective

Edited by

Letty M. Russell, Kwok Pui-lan,
Ada María Isasi-Díaz, Katie Geneva Cannon

The Westminster Press
LOUISVILLE

Book design by Christine Schueler

First edition

Published by The Westminster Press®
Louisville, Kentucky 40202-1396

PRINTED IN THE UNITED STATES OF AMERICA
6 8 9 7

Library of Congress Cataloging-in-Publication Data

Inheriting our mothers' gardens : feminist theology in Third World perspective / edited by Letty M. Russell ... [et al.]. — 1st ed.
    p. cm.
  Bibliography: p.
  ISBN 0-664-25019-X (pbk.)

  1. Woman (Christian theology) 2. Theology, Doctrinal—Developing countries. 3. Feminism—Religious aspects—Christianity.
  I. Russell, Letty M.
  BT704.I64 1988
  230′.088042—dc19   88-10051
                                              CIP

CONTENTS

CONTRIBUTORS

MARTA BENAVIDES is a Salvadoran woman who worked with Archbishop Oscar Romero before his assassination in 1980. An American Baptist minister, she coordinates MEDEPAZ (Ecumenical Ministries for Development and Peace) and has been in a ministry in support of women, labor, peasants, and student groups of her country.

CECILY P. BRODERICK Y GUERRA received her B.A. degree from Trinity College in Hartford, Connecticut, and her M.Div. degree from Berkeley Divinity School at Yale in New Haven, Connecticut. Cecily is a priest in the Episcopal Church serving at St. Philip's Church, New York City. She is a native New Yorker, born of a Jamaican father and a Puerto Rican mother.

KATIE GENEVA CANNON, a radical womanist scholar, is Associate Professor of Ethics at the Episcopal Divinity School in Cambridge, Massachusetts, Visiting Professor at Yale, and an ordained minister

in the Presbyterian Church (U.S.A.). Katie is currently at work on a book about the moral wisdom of Black
women.

CHUNG HYUN KYUNG was born in Korea and
graduated from Ewha Women's University in Seoul
with a B.A. and an M.A. before coming to the United
States for her theological studies. She completed her
M.Div. at the School of Theology at Claremont,
California, and then attended the one-year Study/
Action Program at the Women's Theological Center
in Boston. Currently Hyun Kyung is writing her
Ph.D. dissertation in systematic theology at Union
Theological Seminary, New York City, on "The
Voices of Asian Women in Search of Contextual-
ization in Asian Theologies."

JOANN NASH EAKIN recently returned to Berkeley,
California, after serving as Associate Director of the
Program on Theological Education of the World
Council of Churches in Geneva, Switzerland. Before
that time Joann was Director of the Master of Arts in
Values Program and Associate with the D.Min. pro-
gram at San Francisco Theological Seminary. She is
one of the founders of what has come to be called the
Center for Women and Religion of the Graduate
Theological Union in Berkeley.

ADA MARÍA ISASI-DÍAZ was born in Cuba and
lived there until she was eighteen. Since then she has
lived in three countries and traveled in many others.
Ada is Director of Program and Associate General
Director of Church Women United and sees herself as
a Hispanic feminist activist-theologian committed to
the liberation of Hispanic women. Ada is a doctoral
candidate in social ethics at Union Theological Seminary, New York City. Her first book, written with

Yolanda Tarango and entitled *Hispanic Women: Prophetic Voice in the Church,* was recently published by Harper & Row.

KWOK PUI-LAN is a writer, lecturer, mother, and theologian. She teaches Religion and Society in the Chinese University of Hong Kong and has been active in the ecumenical movement in Asia. Pui-lan has edited *1997 and Hong Kong Theology* and co-edited *Fullness of the Gospel* (both in Chinese). Her articles also appear in *East Asian Journal of Theology* and *Journal of Feminist Studies in Religion.* She is writing her Th.D. dissertation in Religion and Society for Harvard Divinity School on "Chinese Women and Christianity, 1860–1927."

MERCY AMBA ODUYOYE is a Ghanaian Methodist with theological education from the University of Ghana and Cambridge University. She is now working in Geneva with the World Council of Churches as Deputy General Secretary and Staff Moderator of the Program Unit on Education and Renewal. Before going to Geneva, Mercy was a Senior Lecturer in the Department of Religious Studies, University of Ibadan, Nigeria. She has also taught in the United States as a Visiting Lecturer in Women's Studies in Religion at Harvard Divinity School and as the Henry Luce Visiting Professor in World Christianity at Union Theological Seminary, New York City. Her most recent book, *Hearing and Knowing,* published by Orbis Books, is a theological reflection on Christianity in Africa.

LETTY M. RUSSELL is Professor of Theology at Yale Divinity School. She was ordained to the ministry in 1958 by The United Presbyterian Church U.S.A. and served as pastor and educator in the East

Harlem Protestant Parish for seventeen years. Recently she edited the book *Feminist Interpretation of the Bible* and published *Household of Freedom: Authority in Feminist Theology*. She is active in the Commission on Faith and Order of the National Council of Churches and in the World Council of Churches.

INTRODUCTION

In the spring of 1986 some of the women faculty and students at Princeton Theological Seminary gathered together in the Women's Center to discuss plans for holding the fifteenth annual meeting of the Women's Interseminary Conference in April 1987. They wanted a theme that would bring together women of diverse backgrounds.[1] Someone mentioned Alice Walker's description of her mother's way of bringing beauty to the succession of run-down shacks she called home as a child. In her essay "In Search of Our Mothers' Gardens," Walker says:

> I notice that it is only when my mother is working in her flowers that she is radiant, almost to the point of being invisible—except as Creator: hand and eye. She is involved in work her soul must have. Ordering the universe in the image of her personal conception of Beauty.[2]

The group talked about the joys and problems of relationships with their mothers and searched past histories and future hopes for a title. Suddenly,

Renita Weems, an Old Testament graduate student at
Princeton, pointed to the mural that was painted on
the center wall depicting the inheritance of the daughters of Zelophehad in Numbers 36 and saying "Inherit
the Promise." Thus it was that the title of the conference and of this book was born: "Inheriting Our
Mothers' Gardens."

The book began here in the sense that Susan Craig
invited Letty Russell, Kwok Pui-lan, Ada María Isasi-
Díaz, and Katie Cannon as the plenary conversation-
alists, and much of the material in the book was
developed for that ecumenical event. But it is really
the continuation of an ongoing dialogue and friendship among the participants that has developed over a
number of years. Letty has been working with Mercy
Oduyoye on World Council of Churches agendas and
in cooperation with the Ecumenical Association of
Third World Theologians since 1972. Pui-lan worked
with Mercy on the Post-Assembly Core Group, setting
priorities after the Vancouver WCC Assembly. Katie
and Letty both served as pastors at different times in
the same Presbyterian church in the East Harlem
Protestant Parish. Ada María worked with Katie in
writing *God's Fierce Whimsy*.[3] Working in Church
Women United she came to know Marta Benavides.
Marta has been a long-time and long-distance friend
of many of us through a support group in New York
City called the Ad Hoc Group on Racism, Sexism,
and Classism.

Joann has been working with us on programs for
theological education of women in the WCC and also
in San Francisco. Most of us have been involved in
supporting the Women's Theological Center in Boston as well as the Asian Women Theologians, Northeast U.S. Group. The first chairpersons of AWT were
Chung Hyun Kyung and Kwok Pui-lan. Katie has
furthered the dialogue through an annual meeting on
Global Women Theologians in Dialogue at Stony

Point, New York. The networks keep expanding and overlapping, so that those of us involved in this conversation worked together before and enjoyed this chance for continuing dialogue. We believe that our network has to be a global one in which women of all colors, cultures, and continents share their stories of faith and struggle. Our stories here are an invitation to join us in this very local and yet worldwide network.

The title of the book is not without its problems. Many of us do not want to accept our inheritance, either because it represents privilege in background because of race or class, which came to persons like Letty, or because it represents the kind of suffering and oppression documented by Katie. For Ada it is a mixed bouquet, with flowers but also with weeds that need to be relativized or not appropriated. We would venture that this is true for all of us. We all have an inheritance, whether we have claimed it or not, and all of us probably have a mixed inheritance from which we must make critical choices in regard to our own journeys. Most of us need to look for our mothers' inheritance back through history, because we have only known of the inheritance through our fathers. Such research is exciting and lends new vision and energy to our lives, as the stories in this collection attest.

There are similar ambiguities related to "mothers" and "gardens" in the title, but these serve to underlie the richness of the images. Many women have a great deal of difficulty with their mothers because their way of life has changed so radically that their mothers have rejected them. This was emphasized especially by lesbian women at the Women's Interseminary Conference, who said that they had in many ways been cut off from their mothers' gardens. Others find the image of mother evokes only pain, perhaps because they never knew a mother or because their mothers were part of such painful experiences as family violence, alcoholism, divorce, poverty, or sickness. Yet the image of our mothers and grandmothers is often empowering for our lives as we seek to ground faith and action in our own herstory.

In the same way, "gardens" appealed to rural women such as Katie and Marta because they were a source of survival and of beauty, as well as to more affluent women like Letty whose family could afford to grow roses. But for others, like Mercy and Joann, gardens were really cocoa plantations and prairies, or mostly city parks. The gardens, however, became not only descriptions of plots of land but also metaphors for our roots and history and all that has shaped us and our theologies.

Thus the "garden" became an important beginning point for our method of doing feminist theology. For doing theology in a holistic way requires us to include not only our own experiences and stories but also a critical analysis of the effect this has had on our lives, so that we are prepared to understand the stories and the social, political, and historical analysis of those whose lives are quite different from ours, and especially those whose lives are shaped by oppression. The beginning of partnership in dialogue is "digging in your own garden," so that you know what gifts you can bring to the global table talk with your sisters and what parts of your life might be harmful to others. Once we have understood the oppressive and liberating social structures of our own reality more clearly, we are better able to understand the social structures that affect other people's lives. Then we are able to include those data in reflecting on the meaning of the Christian tradition and the clues for liberating action and celebration we find in dialogue with others.

The subtitle, *Feminist Theology in Third World Perspective*, comes from a course at Yale Divinity School where many of the lectures in the book were also shared. The process Katie Cannon and Letty Russell developed in the course for doing theology and ethics in a holistic way is described in Letty's chapter, "From Garden to Table." White women are included with women of color in the subtitle because all of us need to learn what feminist theology means to women from Third World countries and to women of color living in the United States. By listening to the voices of those who have been excluded, and beginning with their oppression and marginality, we may find a way to cultivate a global garden together.

It is clear from our stories that we found this type of "gardening" to be difficult work. Some of us emphasized one part of the task more than another, so we divided the gardening task into three interrelated steps: Claiming Our Mothers' Roots, Clearing Our Space, and Cultivating a Global Garden.

In Part I, "Claiming Our Mothers' Roots," we see that autobiography is an important part of theology, not just an afterthought by way of example or illustration. We have tried to show how stories of our mothers and grandmothers relate to our theological tasks. Sometimes this storytelling is painful and embarrassing, as well as vulnerable to academic scorn. Thus Nellie Wong, an Asian-American writer, says:

> If you sing too often of woe, yours and your sisters', you may be charged with being "too personal," "too autobiographical," too much a woman who cries out, who acknowledges openly, shamelessly, the pain of living and the joy of becoming free.[4]

In spite of these pitfalls, Kwok Pui-lan shows how her story of "Mothers and Daughters, Writers and Fighters" raises new questions and insights for developing an inclusive theology in a Chinese context. Mercy Amba Oduyoye invites us to see how the roots of her African culture are nurtured and made strong through generations of strong and independent women, each calling to the next daughter, "Be a Woman, and Africa Will Be Strong." Chung Hyun Kyung claims the roots of both her birth mother and the mother who raised her. She speaks of "Following Naked Dancing and Long Dreaming" in putting together an indigenous liberation theology for women of faith and struggle in Korean society.

Part II, "Clearing Our Space," provides a warning to all of us that there is a great deal of painful oppression in the stories of women, which has to be dealt with if we are to reconstruct theologies in partnership with one another. For many women, this oppression is still the dominant factor in their story. These women cry, "The harvest is in, but we are not saved."[5] Katie Geneva Cannon underlines this search for survival in a racist world in "Surviving the Blight." Ada María Isasi-Díaz asks for a space within the feminist movement to plant "A Hispanic Garden in a Foreign Land."

Part III, "Cultivating a Global Garden," asks how we might find ways to share in a global garden as partners, rather than as exploiters of one another. This global garden is more of a hoped-for future than a present reality, and we experience it only from time to time as a sign of God's intention for shared community. Joann Nash Eakin tells of her journey "From the Prairie to the World" and of cultivating networks of women in theological education so they can be "encouraged, sustained, and enriched by knowledge of one another's work."

We live from the promise of God for the full liberation of all groaning creation, and in that expectation we seek to cultivate our global garden. In her chapter, "My Mother's Garden Is a New Creation," Marta Benavides depicts the struggle of her Salvadoran people. For Marta, "to know the promise of God is to follow it as a way of life every day and in every struggle." Letty Russell urges us each to begin our cultivation by digging into our own context, so that we will be prepared to move "From Garden to Table," where all people are welcomed to God's feast. And, because gardening is a difficult process that is never finished, Cecily P. Broderick y Guerra has provided us all with an extensive annotated bibliography that becomes required reading for those who want to do feminist theology in Third World perspective.

From time to time in the book there are short letters written in our mothers' tongues. These are love letters that indicate some of the roots we are claiming and cultivating. They tell sisters in different nations about the global garden and their part in the inheritance. In a way this entire book is a love letter, because it expresses the love and commitment all of us have, not only to our own mothers but also to our sisters and their mothers. We invite you to join us in clearing away the blight and making space so that we may all grow into the whole human beings God created!

PART I
Claiming
Our Mothers' Roots

1

Mothers and Daughters, Writers and Fighters

Kwok Pui-lan

I was born in Hong Kong on the twenty-third of March, according to the Chinese lunar calendar. On this day, many Chinese in the coastal provinces of China celebrate the birthday of Mazu, the goddess who protects fisherpeople, seafarers, and maritime merchants. This is also a festive day for my family, for it is the only day in the year that my father will take a day off and go to offer thanksgiving in the temple.

I am the third child of a family of seven children. My mother gave birth to five girls before two sons came at last. Because of the patriarchal and patrilineal structure of the Chinese family, to produce a male heir used to be the most important responsibility of women in marriage. My parents had been waiting for twelve years before the sons were born, and it can be expected that the boys were given most of the attention. From my early childhood, I questioned the legitimacy of a social system that does not treat boys and girls equally.

My mother is tall and thin but very strong. When we were young, we once moved into a new building where the water supply had not yet been adequately installed. To fetch water for the whole family, every day my mother carried two big tins full of water and slowly climbed up seven flights of stairs. This vivid image of her is lodged in my mind. Like many Chinese women of her age, she is a devout follower of folk Buddhist religion. When the moon waxes and wanes, she will offer prayers and thanksgiving sacrifices, and she also makes offerings to the ancestors. When I became a Christian in my teens, my mother did not object to my going to church, and I also thought that she must have found something important in her religious life.

My mother-in-law belongs to an ethnic group called the Kejia, whose women have a reputation of being powerful and independent. Contrary to the prevailing practice, the Kejia women seldom had their feet bound, since many of them had to work in the field. My mother-in-law came from a poor family and was betrothed to her husband as a child. Without learning how to read and write, she has taught herself to make all kinds of things, and her creativity often surprises me. When she lived with us in Hong Kong, she would grow many different vegetables in our backyard during the summer season. Juicy red tomatoes, fleshy white cabbages, and green Dutch beans made our garden look gorgeous. Our little daughter used to help her in watering plants and plucking weeds.

My mother-in-law does not follow any particular religious practice, but she has a profound trust in life and an unfailing spirit to struggle for survival. I have always admired people like my two mothers, who had very limited life chances, yet who have tried to live with dignity and integrity and to share whatever they have with others. The stories of these women have seldom been told, and their lives easily fall into oblivion. Nonetheless, it is these women who pass the wisdom of the human race from generation to generation, and who provide the context of life for others. The stories of my mothers drive home to me a very precious lesson: as women living in a patriarchal cultural system, they are oppressed by men, but, never contented to be treated as victims, they have struggled against the forces that seek to limit them and circumscribe their power.

My Spiritual Foremothers

When I was twelve, one of our neighbors took me to the worship service at an Anglican church. This church is one of two churches in Hong Kong built in a Chinese style, with Christian symbols and motifs embodied in Chinese architecture. I grew to like the liturgical worship, the music, and the fellowship. The vicar of the church was Deacon Huang Xianyun, who was later officially ordained as one of the two women priests in the worldwide Anglican Communion in 1971. Rev. Huang has been a strong role model for me, and her life exemplifies that women can serve the church just as men do.

Rev. Huang has always preached that men and women are created equal before God, and she has encouraged women to develop their potential. Because of her influence, there were many women in our church who volunteered to do various kinds of ministry. As a high school girl, I used to accompany them in visiting the sick and calling on those old people who were too weak to come to church. Some of these women volunteers were widows; a few were rich; others came from poor and middle-class backgrounds. Their dedication to others in ministering to the needy helped me to see glimpses of the divine and sustained me through many doubts and uncertainties.

Just like these women of my church, other Chinese women joined the Christian community in search of an alternative vision of society and human relationships. In the last decades of the nineteenth century, women who joined the church were poor and lower-class; the gentry and the upper-class families would not allow their wives and daughters to follow a foreign religion. To read the Bible and the catechism, these illiterate women had to be taught how to read. Bible-women were employed to translate for the missionaries and to do the home visitations. As the church became involved in social reforms, some of the Christian women participated in literacy campaigns and the anti-footbinding movement and organized health care programs and women's associations.

These activities allowed women to come together to talk about their problems and to find ways and means to tackle them. Amid all the changes in modern China, these women have tried to work for the benefit of women and contribute to society. Like other women in Third World churches, they bear witness to a faith that empowers people to break through silence and move to action. Although many of their names have been lost in history, they are my spiritual foremothers in loving memory.

Between the Two Worlds: As Chinese and as Christian

My double inheritance from my own mothers and my spiritual foremothers has raised a serious question for me: What is the connection between the lives of simple folk like my mothers and Christianity? I have long rejected the arrogance that "outside the church, there is no salvation," for it means condemning my ancestors, mothers, nieces, and nephews. In fact, in the long history of China's encounter with Christianity, the Christian population in China has scarcely exceeded one half of one percent. As a tiny minority, we live among our people in the world's most popu-

lous country, which has a long history and civiliza-
tion. China not only challenges any presumptuous
"universal" salvation history but also presents a world
of thought, language, art, and philosophy radically
different from the Christian tradition. As Chinese
Christians, we have been in constant dialogue with
this rich cultural heritage, long before the term "religious dialogue" was coined.

But to claim that we are both Chinese and Christian
is not an easy matter; in the view of many Chinese,
this claim is simply implausible. Chinese identity is
defined by participation in a complicated cultural
matrix of social behavior, rites, and human relationships, while Christianity is often perceived to be
bound up with Western philosophy, liturgy, and
cultural symbols.[1] Moreover, Christianity came to
China together with the expansion of Western military aggression. We people of Hong Kong are pains-
takingly aware that in the first unequal treaty between
China and the West, Hong Kong was ceded to the
British, and at the same time missionaries were
allowed to preach at China's treaty ports.

With such a heavy historical burden on our shoulders, we Chinese Christians have to vindicate ourselves to our own people: we are not the instruments
of foreign aggressors, nor do we share the same
religion as the oppressors. In the 1920s, religious
leaders in China began the process of the
indigenization of the church, so that Chinese Christians would eventually assume the tasks of self-
propagation, self-support, and self-government. Some
Chinese theologians, at that time, believed that Christianity could be the social basis for the revitalization
of China. Others believed that Christianity could be a
revolutionary force that would lead to social changes.

But as Chinese women, we are much more concerned about how Christianity is indigenized into the

Chinese culture. The Confucian tradition has been
vehemently criticized in China's recent past as advocating hierarchical social relations, strict separation
between the sexes, and a backward-looking worldview. The androcentric moral teachings have been
castigated as undergirding the conservative inertia of
keeping China feudal and patriarchal.[2] At the same
time, Christianity has been subjected to vigorous
dissection and in-depth analyses to expose its dualis-
tic tendency and patriarchal bias.[3] For some time,
Chinese women have taken comfort in knowing that
Jesus advocated equality of the sexes, in spite of the
Jewish patriarchal custom, and that Paul's teachings
on women were limited by the cultural conditions of
his time.[4] But today, Jewish feminists caution us
against anti-Semitic prejudices, and feminist biblical
scholars argue that Paul's bias against women took
place in a much wider process of patriarchalization of
the early church.[5]

In a dazzling way, there is a "shaking of the
foundations" on both sides and we are confronted
with a double culture shock. There is no easy path we
can follow. As one Chinese poet says, "The road is
long and tortuous, we have to search above and
below."[6] Out of this most trying experience, we have
come to face both our cultural heritage and the
Christian tradition with courage and hope, that we
may find new ways to do theology which will liberate
us and sustain our faith.

Searching for a Liberating Faith

The crisis of meaning and identity motivates me to
search passionately for my mothers' gardens. What is
the source of power that they found liberating, and
how were they able to maintain their integrity as
women against all the forces that denied them oppor-

tunities and tried to keep them in a subordinate place? The answer to these questions is not easy to come by, since women's lives have been trivialized and their contributions often erased from our memory. For a long time, the history of Christianity was written from the missionary perspective. These books record the life and work of the missionaries but seldom relate facts about the Chinese Christians. Even when they mention mission for women, they emphasize the work "done for" Chinese women, instead of telling the stories and lives of the women themselves. Chinese scholars, too, have tended to focus more on Chinese men, who could write and therefore leave us with so-called "reliable" historical data. We know too little about the faith and religious imagination of Chinese Christian women.

To be connected with my own roots, I have learned to value the experiences and writings of my fore-mothers. Many of their short testimonies, gleaned from articles in journals and small pamphlets, would not formerly have been counted as "theological data." I have also looked in alternative resources, such as songs, poems, and myths, as well as in unexpected corners, such as obituary notices. Sometimes this requires a fresh treatment of the materials: reading between the lines, attending to small details, and providing the missing links by circumstantial evidence. This meticulous work is done with a deep respect for these women, and in remembrance of their testimony to an alternative understanding of the fullness of life.

Trying to find the link to the threads of their lives, I have come to understand that they were not passive recipients of what was handed down or taught to them. They were brave enough to challenge the patriarchal tradition, both in Chinese culture as well as in Christianity. After they became Christians, some of the women refused to follow the Chinese marriage rites or to participate in the funeral ceremony, which were social enactments of patrilineal and patriarchal family ideals. In addition, some questioned the overt patriarchal bias of the Bible. A Christian woman whose name has been lost to history used a pin and cut out from her Bible Paul's injunction that wives should be submissive to their husbands. When her husband exhorted her to obey what the Bible taught, she brought out her Bible and said it did not contain such teachings. At the turn of this century, a medical doctor named Zhang Zhujun was said to be the first Chinese woman preaching at the church. Commenting on Paul's prescription that women should keep silence in the church, Dr. Zhang boldly asserted that Paul was wrong![7]

About sixty years after Chinese women started to join the church in recognizable numbers, women organized themselves in the first meeting of the Chinese National Council of Churches in 1922. Ms. Ruth Cheng addressed the Assembly and raised the issue of the ordination of women. She said:

> People in some places think that the ordination of women is out of the question and women pastors are simply impossibilities. I do not intend to advocate that the church ought to have women pastors, but I would simply like to ask the reason why women cannot have such rights. If the Western Church because of historical development and other reasons has adopted such an attitude, has the Chinese Church the same reason for doing so? If the ancient Church, with sufficient reasons, considered that women could not have such rights, are those reasons sufficient enough to be applied to the present Church?[8]

These brave acts of women demonstrated their critical discernment, as moral agents, and a radical defiance which uncompromisingly challenged those traditions that were limiting and binding for women.

To claim such a heritage for myself is a process of self-empowerment. First, it informs me that these Chinese Christian women have a history and a story that need to be recovered for the benefit of the whole church. Second, I stand in a long tradition of Chinese Christian women who, with tremendous self-respect, struggled not only for their own liberation but also for justice in church and society. Third, these women brought their experience to bear on their interpretation of Christian faith and dared to challenge the established teaching of the church. It is because of this history that I can claim to do theology from a Chinese woman's perspective.

Toward an Inclusive Theology

There are a few important insights I have found while tending and digging in my mothers' gardens. Their religious experience and quest for liberation point to the necessity of expanding our Christian identity and developing a more inclusive theology. This involves several major shifts in our traditional theological thinking. First, it requires us to shift our attention from the Bible and tradition to people's stories. The exclusiveness of the Christian claim often stems from a narrow and mystified view of the Bible and church teaching. I admit that the Bible records many moving stories of struggle against oppression, and it continues to inspire many Third World Christians today. But I also agree with post-Christian feminists that our religious imagination cannot be based on the Bible alone, which often excludes women's experience.[9] In particular, I cannot believe that truth is only revealed in a book written almost two thousand years ago, and that the Chinese have no way to participate in its inception. Let me give some concrete examples to illustrate what I mean. Coming from the southern part of China, where rice is the main food, I have often found the biblical images of bread-making and yeast-rising as alienating. I also feel a little uneasy when some Western women begin to talk about God as Bakerwoman.[10] The Chinese, who live in an agricultural setting instead of a pastoral environment, have imaged the divine as compassionate, nonintrusive, immanent in and continuous with nature. The images and metaphors we use to talk about God are necessarily culturally conditioned, and biblical ones are no exception.

The Bible tells us stories that the Hebrew people and the Christians in the early church valued as shaping their collective memory. The Western Christian tradition represents one of the many ways to interpret this story for one's own situation. The Indians, the Burmese, the Japanese, and the Chinese all have stories that give meaning and orientation to their lives. Women in particular have a treasure chest of lullabies, songs, myths, and stories that give them a sense of who they are and where they are going. Opening this treasure chest is the first step to doing our own theology. With full confidence, we claim that our own culture and our people's aspiration are vehicles for knowing and appreciating the ultimate. This would also imply that our Christian identity must be radically expanded. Instead of fencing us from the world, it should open us to all the rich manifestations that embody the divine.

Second, we have to move from a passive reception of the traditions to an active construction of our own theology. The missionary movement has been criticized for making Third World churches dependent on churches in Europe and America. This dependence is not just financial but, more devastatingly, theological.

With an entirely different philosophical tradition, we enter into the mysterious debate of homoousia, and with no critical judgment we continue the modernist and fundamentalist debate of the missionaries, long after a partial cease-fire has been declared in the West. We try our best to study Greek and Hebrew, and Latin or German too, if we can manage, and spare little time to learn the wisdom of our own people. As half-baked theologians, we are busy solving other people's theological puzzles—and thus doing a disservice to our people and the whole church by not integrating our own culture in our theology.

All peoples must find their own way of speaking about God and generate new symbols, concepts, and models that they find congenial for expressing their religious vision. We women, who have been prevented from participating fully in this myth- and symbol-making process, must reclaim our right to do so. As a Chinese Christian woman, I have to critically reassess my double heritage, to rediscover liberating elements for building my own theology. Ironically, it is my commitment to feminism that leads me to a renewed interest and appreciation of my own cultural roots. Chinese folk religions have always been much more inclusive, and they do not exclude the female religious image and symbolism. Chinese religious sensibility has a passion for nature and longs for the integration of heaven and earth and a myriad of things. If theology is an "imaginative construction," as Gordon Kaufman says,[11] we would need constantly to combine the patterns and weave the threads in new ways to name ourselves, our world, and our God.

Third, doing our own theology requires moving away from a unified theological discourse to a plurality of voices and a genuine catholicity. The new style of theology anticipates that there will be many theologies, just as there are many different ways of cooking

food. For those who are raised in a cultural tradition
that constantly searches for the "one above many,"
this will imply confusion, complication, and frustration. For others, like me, who are brought up in a
culture that honors many gods and goddesses, this is a
true celebration of the creativity of the people.

The criterion to judge the different styles of theolo-
gizing is not codified in the Bible, and the norm of
theology is not determined by whether it smells
something like that of Augustine and Aquinas—or
Tillich and Barth, for that matter. Instead, it lies in
the praxis of the religious communities struggling for
the liberation of humankind. All theologies must be
judged as to how far they contribute to the liberation
and humanization of the human community. A living
theology tries to bear witness to the unceasing yearn-
ing of human beings for freedom and justice, and
articulates the human compassion for peace and
reconciliation.

Will plurality threaten the unity and catholicity of
the church? For me, unity and catholicity cannot be
understood in terms of religious doctrines and beliefs
but must be seen as an invitation to work together.
Unity does not mean homogeneity, and catholicity
does not mean sameness. Process theologian John B.
Cobb, Jr., captures the meaning of unity well:

> The unity of Christianity is the unity of a historical
> movement. That unity does not depend on any self-
> identity of doctrine, vision of reality, structure of
> existence, or style of life. It does depend on demon-
> strable continuities, the appropriateness of creative
> changes, and the self-identification of people in rela-
> tion to a particular history.[12]

The particular history that Third World people and
other women's communities can identify with is that
God is among the people who seek to become full
human beings. Today, as we Third World women are

doing our own theology, we come closer to a unity that is more inclusive and colorful and a catholicity that is more genuine and authentic.

I heartily welcome this coming age of plurality in our way of doing theology, that our stories can be heard and our experiences valued in our theological imagination. To celebrate Asian women's spirit-rising, I would like to conclude by sharing a song written by my dear friend Mary Sung-ok Lee:[13]

WE ARE WOMEN

We are women from Burma, China,
India, Japan, Korea, Malaysia,
Philippines, Thailand, and U.S.A.

> *Chorus:* Eh hey ya ho-o
> Eh hey ya ho-o
> Cho ku ṇa cho wa (Oh, how good it is'
> Eh hey ya ho-o.

We are women, we are alive,
breaking our silence,
seeking solidarity.

> *Chorus*

We are women, Yellow women,
angered by injustice,
denouncing exploitation.

> *Chorus*

We are sisters, gathered for bonding,
mothers and daughters,
writers and fighters.

> *Chorus*

We are women, spirit-filled women,
claiming our story,
voicing our poetry.

> *Chorus*

路漫漫其修遠兮
吾將上下而求索   《離騷》

　　我們對信仰的追尋，是漫長
而曲折的道路。
　　中國的信徒婦女，在過去的
日子，曾經向壓迫婦女的社
會制度和宗教思想提出挑戰，
她們參加了反纏足運動、婦女
節制會，及女青年會的工作。
　　今天，我們要學效她們的
模範，批判地繼承傳統中
國文化和基督教思想，深入
地發展有中國特色的婦女神
學，與第三世界婦女一起，為人
類整體的釋放，作出貢獻。

郭佩蘭
八七、十二．

2

Be a Woman,
and Africa Will Be Strong

Mercy Amba Oduyoye

DREAM GIRL DREAM

What's the future going to be?

Dream girl dream.
What we may become, that's what matters.

Dream woman dream.
Woman dream, Africa's dream.

Dream of the least of the world,
Permissible dreams.

Dream, for the other is you turned inside out.

Make the other strong and you will be strong,
We shall all be strong together.
Dream girl dream.

Be a woman, and Africa will be strong.

Yes, I live in a dream world, because in me the past and the future have come together. I have the memory of the future my grandmother and my mother put before me; I live out this future while creating a future for myself. "You will be a mother of twins," said my grandmother. "No, not before you can stand on your own feet do you allow a man into your life," said my mother. A mother of many and one that carries her own head: that is me in the future. So I saw and still work for a future in which caring for the other becomes a way of life—no, more than that, a way of being myself, maybe even a mother of twins. I embody a tension that makes me creative and free, a being that is giving birth to herself from the matrix of a mother-centered community.

My Story

Living out of my Christianized Akan background, I have never ceased to dig around that culture in search of my mother's specifically Asante and Brong backgrounds, the side of my family that was not as completely sold on Christianity as other branches seemed to be. It was exciting to discover my Asenie blood, linked with that of the priest-politician Okomfo Anokye, who helped unify the Asante into a strong nation.[1] I knew then I had in my veins the blood of mothers who would not be ordered around, not even by illustrious sons of the clan, brothers whose inheritance their children, being nephews, would claim. I knew then that my mothers would mother and honor and serve only the men they chose to espouse—not men *as* men. They gave their all to those whom they, the mothers, considered worthy. The language about Asenie women is far from evoking images of softness. We have been called tough and determined (*anioden,* "hard-eyed"). We have been called witches (*moyere,* "you emit the night light"). We have been called daring (*modue bo*). In my veins flows the blood of Abena Gyata, the mother of the Asenie.[2] My mothers were leaders, caring and compassionate, self-motivated, and strong of will and character.

Blood may be myth, genes too scientific, but there is nothing like a story to help fix one's self-image. I love stories, myths, folk tales, proverbial sayings, and songs. All that is memorable and "tellable" does shape us, subtly but also deeply, intensely, and more thoroughly and permanently than one is led to imagine. Even though I have not grown up among my mother's mothers, there was enough of them left in her and in the stories she told. Westernization could not rob her of the stories of her mothers. Neither could Christianity lead her to demean her ancestry. I could not help but catch the spirit, in her and in the stories she told. Through the years of kitchen tales and the admonitions of the do's and don'ts of womanhood, my mother sowed in me the seeds that have made me an Asenie woman.

I was particularly blessed with much that was Asante in tone. My feminist heritage was heightened not only by being my mother's daughter but also by growing up in the Asante and Brong areas in Ghana, where my parents served the Methodist Church. Any conscious upbringing I had was aimed at making me a lover of the church and grateful to God for being who I am: an African woman who is a Christian. Coming from God, all this background was treated as a gift and a challenge, the context in which to live a full and beautiful life, as a Christian woman closely attached to the church because her parents and her grandparents knew nothing else.

The gardens of the mission houses I was brought up in were tended by hired hands, and so were those of the elite schools I attended. They were not my mother's gardens. Yet in another real sense I have soil on my hands.

My own life began in the context of a colonial

economy. To provide a cash crop with which to enter
Western culture, the British had promoted cocoa
farming in the then Gold Coast. Every bar of chocolate still reminds me of the story of my arrival on the
world scene. It was a Saturday. My mother had
walked some five miles, a pregnant woman among a
long line of persons of all ages on a forest track, going
in single file to my grandfather's farm. In the harvest
season everyone is busy. The first stage in the production of chocolate for the women of Europe begins on a
cocoa farm.

The yet-to-be-born Amba was not to be left out of
this communal effort to get the family into a Western
economy. I arrived in the middle of the harvest, the
first fruit of my mother's womb. On my eighth day on
earth, I was given the name Amba Ewudziwa: Amba
for being a girl born on Saturday and Ewudziwa after
my grandfather, Kodwo Ewudzi. My grandfather
planted a special yam on the farm to mark my birth.

That mother and daughter survived this unortho-
dox arrival has always fueled my faith. Why did I
survive? That I do not know, but I know *how* I
survive. I have faith in the future of the African
woman and her power to transform Africa.

To articulate my own faith has meant being faithful
to the church and to the faith by which my father
lived, but doing it in the way his mother and my
mother lived it.[3] Mine is a faith that mothers both self
and others, for I can only love others to the extent that
I love myself. From such a feminist ancestry, and with
a father who believed in teasing out the good in all he
encountered, I could not help but develop a self-
awareness that put me in the company of those of my
age-mates who questioned the basis of authoritative
statements. My experience meant something; it cannot be pushed aside. Finding myself in the camp of
liberation theologians and Christian feminists was as
natural to me as claiming the priesthood of Okomfo

Anokye, the self-determination of his sisters, and the coordinating ability of Abena Gyata. This woman could not have been a leader if she had not been perceptive and compassionate, bold, persistent, and accountable to the group for its well-being.

I do my theology and advocacy thinking of the roles my paternal grandmother and my mother played in the church; my father could not have served as model, even if the church were to ordain women. I am too much of an Asenie woman; to cultivate the strength of his selflessness would make me a different person altogether. I have to suck the nutrients for my theology out of the breasts of my mothers, whose experience of the church and of life is closer to mine.

My mother and the women of her age group knew Westernization to varying degrees. They lost their names and were expected to merge their identities with those of their husbands. Their resistance is in itself a struggle to be thankful for. They took their husbands' names but did not lose their own specific identities. It is to them we owe the partial failure of the patriarchalization of what was a mother-centered culture; left to men, the "damage" would have been total. Without the resistance put up by my mother's generation, our contemporary struggle would have been even more herculean. My age group and those after us have followed their lead in accepting Westernization only to the extent that it suits us: only to the extent that it does not subjugate or jeopardize what we see as belonging to the gospel of Jesus. What is specifically Christian is irresistible. But Christianity in Africa began by confusing Christianity and European culture.

The West and My Mothers

In Africa the church is the most overt manifestation of Christianity. However, Christianity has also done so much enculturation through Westernization that women who are not Christians are, by the very fact of being affected by Western culture, under the church's influence. The most obvious example of this enculturation is found in the patriarchalization of African family life. Let me illustrate from the groups I experience personally: the Yoruba (through my husband's family in Nigeria), and the Akan (through my family in Ghana), using their system of naming persons.

Generally speaking, you can tell where in Ghana or in Nigeria an individual comes from and may even be able to name the province, if not a specific town. You can tell even by the marks on the face. People are named not after fathers but in such a way as to identify them with a larger group of people. Fathers' names are not handed down to mark who "sires" an individual; such surnames are a Western imposition. People in Africa who had to deal with Westerners and their structures and religion acquired surnames by the simple process of adding the second name of their father to their first name or sometimes to their two or more names. Thus the four brothers of my father all became Yamoah and passed that name on to their wives and children. The whole ideology and the theology of naming was transformed by this one demand that the African have a surname like the European. African women found themselves transformed from persons identified by their parents to husband attachments that were unknown before and whose import Africa has never accepted in its totality.

Westernization of this sort was promoted through church schools and church membership, but it was also required of all others who came into contact with the so-called modern sector. Here we will look specifically at the church, bearing in mind that it functioned —and, to a large extent continues to function—as part of Westernization.

The gardens that I dig stretch at least through five generations of Methodist churchwomen from Ghana. The first generation would be a grandmother (Nana) who now would either be dead or over a hundred years old, for she represents women in the church who were mature enough to have children in the first decade of this century. The second generation (Mama) would be now between the ages of sixty and eighty and would have children who are in their forties and fifties. These daughters would be Mmasirwa; this midpoint is my generation, the third. The fourth generation, daughters of Mmasirwa, under forty, would be Nneemafo, modern women. Their daughters, the fifth generation, would be Mmabaawa and would be in their late teens or early twenties. Over these hundred years, Nana, Mama, Mmasirwa, Nneemafo, and Mmabaawa all experienced different phases of Christianization and different intensities of Westernization. Their levels of participation in the church's life also differ and, of course, overlap across the years. I shall deal briefly with each generation, choosing what is most characteristic.

Nana

Nana was born in the late nineteenth century, became Christian (or had Christian parents), and lived in a period in West African history when the church was a new and fresh approach to spirituality worth trying. Coming from a primal religion that was hospitable enough to grant the validity of other approaches to God, Christianity was simply another such approach. Most in this age group would be first-generation converts. For most of West Africa the church is less than two hundred years old, though Christianity is older on the coast. Nana would either be farming in a rural area or involved in the fish trade

from a fishing village demanding long-distance traveling to periodic markets.

My own grandmother did wholesale and retail
trading of fish in an inland town, Asamankese; her
suppliers were her sisters, who had remained in the
fishing town of Apam. They belonged to the royal
house there and never became reconciled to her
moving away, since she was the eldest woman. My
grandmother, whom everyone called Maame, also
traded in household goods associated with the West,
such as china and cutlery. She was the first baker in
town and also made beads. The market was Maame's
domain, and even a little child could take you to her
stall.

The women of Asamankese and the surrounding
villages who were farmers also brought their food-
stuffs to the market on a daily basis, but Thursday was
market day, and women came from a forty-mile
radius and farther.[4] The farmers bringing produce
would bring their crafts, mainly pottery, just as the
fish trader would also be carrying beads and salt from
the coast. Nobody traveled alone; every woman would
be accompanied by a girl carrying wares and learning
the trade who would someday take it over. It is from
our grandmothers that we have inherited the West
African Market, an outstanding women's institution
that serves more than commercial purposes.

The language of commerce would also be the language of the gospel, for right there in the marketplace
an enthusiastic convert to the new religion would be
announcing the "good news" of a new religion whose
chief character was called Jesus (Christ), a child of
God and Wonder-Worker. This might be Nana's first
contact with the new religion. Subsequently she might
hear it through interpretation from the words of a
white man or some other *opotoni* ("one who does not
speak an intelligible language"). Either way, the gospel was a story told. If Nana was convinced and,

against all odds and even in the face of persecution, was baptized, she too learned the story and retold it.

In the Methodist Church Ghana, a tradition of lyrical rendering of the gospel stories grew out of the Fanti primal worship and became the women's response to preaching. From the start the majority of the preachers and exhorters were men; so were the few who could read. The women absorbed the stories, committing to memory chapter and verse of what they heard, read, or were told through preaching. This provided the repertoire from which they wove the lyrics they sang.

To relate to the reality to which African women respond, you must hear them pray. Women today continue in this tradition, weaving everyday concerns with biblical paradigms and singing them at gatherings for worship. Men do "raise" lyrics, but it is primarily a women's culture in Methodist Church Ghana.[5] Sometimes the preacher would request this musical interlude, and the cantor would come up with the appropriate biblical story or ethical response. But more often than not the cantor would simply interrupt the preacher with the interlude in the monologue, telling all that needed to be told on the theme through a song which the people, having taken part in its singing, would carry with them for a long while. The gospel was a spoken word—heard, believed, and retold. A word in season is like a timely lyric.

Some of these women would have learned to read their mother tongue in Sunday school and could thereby eliminate the mediation of the "reader," who almost always was a man. The gospel would then cease to be a man's word to a gathered community and become a direct word from God to the woman who was reading for herself. But read or heard, there was very little in the language of the Fanti Bible that would make Nana feel excluded.

The church was a new cult that happened to have a

man as the link to God and men as its cultic functionaries. Nana did not question this; neither did anyone
question the African cults that were men-only or
women-only at the top. When a male diviner speaks it
is the voice of the god that is heard, and the fact that
the medium is a man does not give men any special
privileges in the communication between humans and
the spirit world.

The divinity could be male but there was no direct
correlation between spirituality and maleness as far as
the spirit world was concerned and no direct link
between being male and being divine; several of the
spirit beings in African cults were female. Nana
therefore had no problem with the all-male Christian
clergy and gave them no significance beyond their
being functionaries. Serving God does not make one
God.

As a Methodist woman, Nana could be the class
leader of an all-female Society Class, leading Bible
study, helping others to understand Methodist discipline, and raising funds to support the church. She
would go to the leaders' meeting every Thursday, as
did all the male class leaders. Unisex organization was
the accepted norm in African society.

My grandmother and her age-mates had their children baptized with Christian names and surnames, as
demanded by the church and the colonial government, and sent them to mission schools. They con-
firmed them in church and married them off in
church. At every stage, traditional rites of passage
were also followed, to the degree that the people kept
in touch with being Akan. Some aspects of traditional
rites were modified.

The flexibility and the creativity of African cultic
functionaries is demonstrated by these new rites that
evolved to cope with the Christian presence. By the
second decade of this century, mature women were

already taking part in telling the gospel story and preparing their daughters to do the same and to go even further, because they had acquired the new skills of reading and even writing. Nana and her age group often functioned in the church even though they had no official designation or status; they were no less effective than the men, who wore titles of Sofo, Alufa, Pastor, Reverend, teacher, and catechist.

Their children, born just before and during World War I, are my mother's generation. They, in turn, became parents in the 1930s and 1940s. My maternal grandmother, Awo Yeboaa, passed on while my mother, Yaa Dakwaa, was still a baby. The grandmother whose words I hear even now is my paternal grandmother, Maame Awotwiwa (Mrs. Martha Yamoah). She features in my own style, as I have appropriated the oral transmission of scripture and theology in the specific form of lyrics and taken over the interventionist style that refuses to honor ex-cathedra monologues.

Mama

Unlike earlier generations, a few of the women in my mother's age group received a formal education, mostly through the elitist educational system set up by the missions. Some may even have had additional training to equip them to become wives of pastors and teachers. The younger ones of this generation may have been educated as teachers, and a handful became nurses and midwives.

More would become class leaders but not leaders in the formal liturgy. These women were almost weaned from lyric interventions, which came to be seen as a form of expression appropriate only for those who could not speak English. For my mother and her age-mates, becoming Westernized was seen as the road to

liberation from African sexism. They threw themselves into the church; the missionary's wife was their
model. Women's work would have given them additional meeting days devoted to specific women's concerns as distinct from the church's concerns discussed
at class meetings.

These women also gave their energy and time to
youth work among young girls, which developed
before the church thought it was necessary to "social-
ize" young men to Christianity. They were the main-
stay of the church's finances and joined in the
communal labor that built churches and schools.
African churchwomen's groups have always done
these things without questioning. They were seeing to
God's work, convinced that God would see to their
needs.

None questioned the church's discipline or the
white male image of the liturgical leadership. When,
after World War II, African male leadership began to
emerge in church in spite of racism, paternalism
meant that the women were not included. African
Charismatic churches began to boom, but even here
the leadership was mostly male. Women's leadership
across the board was meager at the level of "the final
say," but women saw no reason to complain. So
Mama carried more responsibility in the church without getting any more authority than Nana had and
maybe even less, because Westernization was teaching
Africa the advantages of keeping women invisible.

My mother entered completely into my father's life,
sharing his ministry and taking seriously women's
supportive role in the church. This was a team ministry, although it was not recognized as such. They
agreed that their children and future generations were
a trust; they should be directed but not molded into
the image of the passing age group. Times were
changing rapidly. What the coming generation needed
was to have their innate charisma enhanced.

Mmasirwa

Mama had her daughters in the 1930s and 1940s. There were more opportunities for formal education, and many had a college education. Although you may not find a doctorate in religion among them, in other fields they have not done so badly. The sacrifices of my mother and her age-mates for their daughters' education paid off, and today's *mmasirwa,* even if unordained, are a very potent force in the church. None can afford to ignore them. The church, of course, is far behind other fields of Western education, training, and employment. While African women in other areas have served with men and reached and passed retirement age, the oldest woman in the theological discipline is yet to turn sixty, and every new doctorate is like a breath of fresh air. The role models are finally being created. A new day is about to dawn for the African woman and for the church to which she belongs.

Few of my age-mates have taken to the church beyond their mothers' generation. In fact, in proportion, one could say their participation is declining in formal and official church circles. They have little time to give to the church to misuse. Effective participation has therefore become static at the level of Mama's generation. Still no one questions, for the role models, such as they are, are outside Africa. The church has fitted perfectly into the predominant patriarchy that the West has come to reinforce.

Nneemafo

To raise the issue of ordination or to point to some of the obvious exclusions of women is to be an imitator of the degenerate West. Never mind that the Charismatic African churches have women in key places. They do not constitute a model for the Western churches to which most of the Westernized women belong. They have had their daughters, who are now in their late twenties and early thirties. These women will simply ignore the churches if the churches ignore their charisms. This is the Nneemafo, young women with doctorates in theology who are teaching or doing research.

Among the Nneemafo are theologians whose voices I echo in my work and from whom I learn what is close to the hearts of the two generations after me. Nneemafo are found in all walks of life, and those who are churchwomen expect to see women in the ordained ministry. Those studying theology aspire to the highest degrees through university programs or to ordination through church-owned seminaries and colleges. They know that barriers are set up to frustrate them and that religion is often the most damaging of those barriers. Both they and I know that we must focus relentlessly on the religio-cultural factors that affect Christian women and Christian theology.

Mmabaawa

The slogan "Equity 2000" may not apply to the African churchwoman, but the teenage girls studying religion in the high schools, the Mmabaawa, have role models that were not available to me. I am convinced that African churchwomen will go into ministries that will speed up the day when "if the bean falls to the ground it would be split into two equal halves." With the strong tradition of sisterhood in Africa there is no limit to what women there can do to teach the church the meaning and practice of ministry. The girls of today who observe the new image of women theologians are already reimaging what the participation of women in the church might be. By the time today's Mmabaawa enter their twenties and thirties, we shall have a new theological scene shaped by the awareness of all that thwarts community. I live in anticipation of this and theologize today according to this dream of tomorrow.

My Theology

I have tried to indicate the spirit of confidence and sense of being a participant that my grandmothers gave me. We are human because we are jointly responsible with others for what happens to our community. In a community a person's word must be heard and evaluated alongside that of others. Gender is no criterion for the lack or possession of wisdom. As Abena Gyata led the Asenie and as Maame Awotwiwa, my grandmother, contributed to Christianization in her generation, so I have a duty to help forge a relevant theology for a living Christianity in Africa.

As they knew the paths to their destination and the elements in the past to take along, so I attempt to search the gardens of my culture for what is Christ-like, and liberating, and therefore worth lifting up as a manifestation of the Spirit of God at work among my people. My grandmothers carried their own heads, so I cannot but carry my own head too, together with others, as we seek new forms of partnership beyond the bifocal structures I find insufficient for crafting a liberating community.

Carrying your own head is not the same as naming yourself (the latter is autonomous). It is a concept that implies listening to the community and letting your self-determination be shaped by a vision of its ideals. It implies a self-discipline that does not rule out compromise a priori, because if there is a genuine process of consensus one's views and one's welfare will not be trampled. I can operate outside my Akan community and live. But I cannot be alive in a community that ignores my existence. Much of what I

have written so far has had this community orientation, either explicitly as a subject or implicitly in my
approach.

The women of the Christian community symbol-
ized by my grandmother and my mother are not only
an inspiration, they are a guide, and sometimes they
function as monitors of what I write. I feel accountable to them as someone expected to carry on a
tradition of ensuring life-centeredness in the community. As teenagers, we young people growing up in the
mission house used to call the prominent women of
the church "the women who have the say-so." We
sensed their influence in the society and in the church
even when we did not understand the structures that
affected how everything was run.

They were not ministers, but we knew they "owned
the church." It was their dedication and their faith in
the church's "worthwhileness" that kept me with the
church despite my awareness of its patriarchal nature
and sometimes blatant discrimination against wom-
en. I have sought to articulate what my grandmother
acted out in her lyrics: announcing the word of God is
not exclusively a man's enterprise. To this I have
added my mother's quiet insistence that a person
owes her community nothing less than her best, but
she cannot give her best if she is not empowered to do
so. It is an unforgivable act to stop a person midstream simply on the basis of gender. Luckily for me,
my father shared this view of human development.

My church-mothers were leaders of women first and
of their community only by extension. But I have
never forgotten my Asante-mothers who led groups of
people. The only limit I recognize in myself is how
well I can perform. But it is a limit that the
patriarchally organized church discounts, having set
up limits based on gender; it also decrees that one has
to be commissioned, appointed by the community,
and designated to perform specific church tasks.

The academy, in this regard, is a little less sexist, especially where employment is concerned. African governments have proven themselves less male-oriented than the Christian church. I have found myself for twelve years earning my living from the university while serving the church in voluntary capacities and using the same gifts. This is no accident. My church-mothers before me did that.

Churches have been known to insist that wives of ministers do no other work but assist in the ministry of their husbands. They employ two people for the salary of one. Women's charisma is valued and utilized by churches as long as it is offered gratis. My mothers accepted this. I do not. So then why have I done so for so much of my life? I have in my own theology made the difference between sacrificing and being sacrificed. The church offers up too many women on the altar of patriarchy. But there are women who consciously and deliberately stay with the church, struggling to live out the future in the oppressive present. Theirs is a living and life-enhancing sacrifice.

The Akan have a proverb, *Wonnkoo obi afum a wose wonko na woye okuafo.* It is a way of saying that you gain a better perspective of the kind of farmer you are if you visit other people's farms. The tendency to become myopic is not only a personal one. Churches and universities tend to think they have the clearest views of the future of the human community. A woman in these structures can feel condemned to isolation. For a woman doing theology this can be devastating, because it tends to make her an oddity. It is like being an Elijah in the midst of all the priests and prophets of the patriarchal Baal.

Stepping into other women's farms was like being born into a fresh and nurturing culture. From this global perspective all my mothers began to make sense. They all expressed a single theme: "Be a woman. Seek and work only for what is life-sustaining. Don't just change with the times, let the times change because you are present. Make a difference." It is their faith and hope, their courage and strength, their joy and their love that connect me with myself and move me to connect with all who love life and seek to make a difference. So I do my theology always asking, "What difference does it make?" And I do a lot of dreaming, anticipating today the Gospel future. The twins of what is and what is yet to be still struggle within me. Yet already the new African woman and theologian is on the threshold. The waters of her coming are already gushing out; with her comes the water of life.[6] So the gardens shall bloom. Only the flowers and the vegetables shall be allowed to live; weeds and blight shall be forbidden.

Menuanom Mmea,

Ɔman Ghana abakɔsɛm kyerɛ yɛn sɛ mmea animdefo, akokudurifo ne ayanyefo pii kaho na etintim ɔman yi fapem. Asantefo tetesɛm ka sɛ mmaapayin baaason na ɛkyekyeree mmusuakuw ason a ɛwɔ Asanteman mu. Mmea nyansa na ɔkora yɛn amanne ahorow pii. Wɔyɛ ɔbea na ade to woa wodi. Adunsifo, akuafo, adwontofo ne aguadifo akɛse akɛse pii yɛ mmea. Eyi nti nsem a mɔakyerɛw no borɔfo mu a ɛfa Akanfo mmea ho nyinaa kɔsi sɛ, mmea na ɔman yie yɛ gyina wɔn so. Nea mepɛ mahu ara ne sɛ, nnɛɛmmafo mmea bɛbɔ wɔnho piriw na wɔbɛhyɛ ɔman Ghana ne Abibiman nyinaa animuonyam.

Sɛ Kristosom betim wɔ ɔman yi mu a, ne kɛse fi mmea. Yɛn nenanom na ɛgyee Asɔre too mu, de wɔn ahoɔden ne wɔn bere boaa Asɔfo. Nso kan no na mmarima nko na wɔhyɛ wɔn asɔfo. Eyi anhaw abibifo mmea. Onyame mmere na ɛyɛ, nnɛ yɛ wɔ mmea asɔfo wɔ kristo asafo horow pii mu. Ɛfata saa ara, efisɛ mmere dan wo a wodan wo ho. Yɛn ara Akanfo na yɛbubɛ sɛ 'Nipa nyina yɛ Onyame mma' ɛna Kristofo so gyedi sɛ nipasu yɛ Onyanesu. Enti sɛ wobua onipa animtiaa na wɔtia Onyame. Wɔn a wɔde mmea anim sesew fa mu no were fi sɛ onipa biara fata animuonyam a Onyame de ahyɛ adasammaa.

Eyi nti sɛ wo ba bea pɛ sɛ ɔyɛ nkɔɔso dwuma a hyɛ no nkuran. Bɛ a wobu no sɛ 'Ɔbea tenten so abɛ a ɔtɔtam di' no de, mma emfi w'anum sɛ woderehyɛ abeawa biara abagow. Ma ɛmpaw wo sɛ wobɛyɛ huntiw dua ama mmeawa a wɔpɛ sɛ wɔyɛ ɔnyame dwuma. Menuanom mmea, asaase yi so de yɛbedii nsɔboa. Yɛn nenanom ne yɛn nanom aye bi. Nkyirimma mmea monsɔre ɛ! Amba Ewudziwa.

3
Following Naked Dancing and Long Dreaming
Chung Hyun Kyung

"Mom, stop it!"

I screamed at her, but she did not look at me. She continued her dance, moving nearly naked in the forest. I felt ashamed of her; I wished she were not my mother. There was nothing to hide the scene before me. There was a deathly silence around us, except for Mother's singing and the sound of the river.

Under the hot sun of August, the forest seemed to be taking a nap. There were no villagers moving about, only Mother and I. She looked like a person who did not belong to this world. I saw real happiness in her face while she was singing and dancing. I could see her breasts, the lines of her body—large, like a whale's—through her wet underwear. I did not want anybody in the world to see that shape, my mother's body that had worked and lived. I finally started to cry out of extreme embarrassment. I wanted to hide from her. She did not look anymore like the noble mother of whom I was always proud. But in spite of my crying, she continued singing and dancing, twirling in the forest as a child might, twirling and dancing in a space of her own.

This happened twenty-four years ago, when I was seven. My mother and I were traveling together to visit her older sister, who lived in a small, remote village in a southern province in Korea. My father was deeply involved with his business and had remained at home in Seoul. I had been raised in a big city, and traveling to a remote village was not easy for me. No bus or train service was available. We had to go over the mountain and cross the river. I was exhausted from walking so long on the dusty road under a hot summer sun. Mom had been telling me stories from her childhood as we were walking—how she had played in the river and climbed the mountain with her sisters. So when we came to the river, Mother's memories came to life and she took off her clothes and started to bathe in the water. She encouraged me to bathe with her. I was shocked. How could she do this? I looked to see whether there were any other people around. No one was there. I did not approve of my mother's behavior at all. I hoped she would finish her bathing as soon as possible. I sat on the riverbank and waited.

At last she got out of the water, but the situation only grew worse. She began singing a song I had never heard before. She danced while she was singing. I thought my mother had gone crazy; otherwise she would never have acted like that. Humiliation and confusion made me cry. "Mom, stop it, *stop it!*" I screamed, but she continued to dance and sing, her body flopping and straining against the dampened clothes. I could not stop the tears from coming, and we stayed like that—me crying and her dancing—for some time. After a while, because of my continuous crying, she stopped her dance and put on her clothes and we took up our journey again.

One Mother's Story

Most of the time my mother behaved like a typical Korean housewife. She took care of us very well. She saved all the best parts of food for my father and me, eating the leftovers herself. She appeared to be submissive to my father and made many sacrifices on behalf of both of us. But there was a contradiction in her life. From time to time, her behavior showed a wild, raw, extreme passion for freedom that was not characteristic of the model Korean woman. The contradiction that she lived she also taught me. The manner in which she raised me was very different from other Korean mothers. Even though she kept telling me to be a "nice" likable girl, she never asked me to cook for family gatherings or feasts, which is the Korean girl's family duty. Rather, she would give me a small amount of money and tell me to go to the library to study whenever the big feasts came. She always told me that I could learn how to cook any time I wanted, but I could not learn how to study once I became older. Sometimes she scolded me because she thought I was too tomboyish. She frequently told me that if I was not feminine, I would not get married because no man would want me. But at other times, she seriously told me not to get married. She said I could not live a full life in marriage because marriage, for a Korean woman, meant giving up freedom.

I still vividly remember the night I had a serious fight with my college boyfriend over the issue of marriage. I loved him very much, but I could not jump into the marriage, as he was insisting, because I had strong doubts about the limitations it would place on my freedom. I could not live without freedom. He accused me of being a selfish woman. I came home crying after a bitter argument with him and had a long conversation with Mother. After listening to my story, she leaned toward me in utter seriousness and offered her advice.

"Hyun Kyung," she said, "do not get married. I have been married for more than forty years. Marriage works for the man, but not for the woman. Forget about your boyfriend. Korean men don't understand women. Live fully. If you want to do something very much—from your heart, from your gut— then do it. Don't hesitate. If you don't have money, then make money, even if it means selling your used underwear. Discipline yourself to be a good scholar when you are young, since you always have loved to learn." And she added, with ambivalence, "Go abroad to study. And if, while you are studying, you find a good *Western* man who can understand *you,* your inner life, then get married. *Western* men seem more generous to women than Korean men."

I was very surprised by my mother's response. I could not believe what she had said. Her advice to me contradicted my image of her as a model Korean woman, someone who worried that I might not get married, who scolded me for my "unfemininity."

My mother passed away one year after I arrived in the United States to begin my theological studies. I cried in my bed every night for more than six months after she died, missing her—missing her like a little motherless child. I felt as if I were standing by myself in the middle of a wilderness, struggling with a powerful storm. My mother had gone; it was the loneliest time in my life.

The Other Mother's Story

Three years after my mother's death, I returned to Korea. There I heard about the existence of my other mother from my cousin-sister. She told me that I had a birth mother besides my late mother. I could not believe it.

If it were true, how could it be that I had never heard about her? If it were true, it would mean that my late parents had totally deceived me. Even in their last words, my father and mother did not mention her to me. If I really did have another mother, a birth mother, then this woman had been erased from my family history, totally erased for the entire thirty years of my life.

My cousin-sister took me to meet my other mother. With confused emotions, I silently followed her until we came to the door of my other mother's home just outside the city of Seoul. I had brought a dozen red roses with me to give to my other mother. I stood at her doorway, holding the roses, and timidly reached for the doorbell.

An old woman opened the door. When she saw me her eyes filled with tears. She took my hands in her own and asked, "Is this Hyun Kyung?" I said, "Yes." Then she began to sob. She told me, "Finally I have met you! I thought I would die without seeing you. Now I can leave this world without holding my *han*."[1]

I did not even know how I felt. I felt numb. Without knowing how to respond, I listened to her story.

My mother was a Korean version of a surrogate mother. In Korea, we call these women *ci-baji*. *Ci* means seed, *baji* means receiver. Therefore, the literal meaning of *ci-baji* is "seed receiver."[2] According to my birth mother, my late mother could not conceive a child even after twenty years of marriage. My father became very anxious. He wanted to have *his* own child in order to continue *his* family line. So he asked my late mother to search for a *ci-baji* woman for him. My late mother found a woman from the countryside who was a *yu-mo*[3] for a child in our neighborhood. My father, however, did not like her at all; he thought she was not bright and beautiful enough to be a *ci-baji* for *his* future child. He sent her away and began to look for a *ci-baji* himself. He found a woman he liked, a woman who had lost her husband during the Korean War. She lived with her mother. My father followed her for a few months and finally persuaded her to conceive a baby for him. She and my father had posed for a picture when they knew that she had become pregnant, and she showed that picture to me. She was a good, healthy-looking woman. She gave birth to me and raised me until my first birthday.

The day after my first birthday, my parents came to my birth mother's house and took me from her. She did not want to let me go, but she could not challenge my parents. They were economically and politically powerful in her city. So she had to give me up, and I, of course, soon forgot her.

She became mentally disordered for a while because of her intense feelings of helplessness and sadness. Even when she recovered from the mental disorder, she could not regain her physical strength for a long time. She said she spent more than a year crying and missing her child. My parents had commanded her not to see me until I had married and borne my first child.

My father was kind to her, but my mother was not. Once my birth mother visited my parents' home because she missed me so much, but my mother did not even allow her to enter the house. My birth mother kept a record of the days of my life. She showed me an old photo album. Surprisingly enough, there I was, first as an infant, a student, and at other stages of my life. She said my father had sent her photos of me, and she kept them carefully. She had watched me and prayed for me for thirty years. They were prayers offered from the shadow of history.

She had inquired after my well-being in various ways. She knew what happened to me in my primary school, high school, and college years. She asked people who had gone to school with me about my activities, but always without revealing her relationship to me. She deliberately did not make herself known to me in order not to hurt my feelings or jeopardize my future. In Korean tradition, children who are born by a *ci-baji* woman are not considered legitimate; they are like second-class children. In the Yi Dynasty, which lasted until the dawn of the twentieth century in Korea, those who were born of a surrogate mother could not take exams to hold governmental offices.[4] This tradition still thrives in Korean society today, although in a subtle way. That is why she did not want to reveal herself to me. She remained hidden for my sake.

I stayed with her for two days before returning to the United States. When she fell asleep, I looked into her face. White hair and many wrinkles told me of her hard life's journey. In her face, I met all Korean women who had been erased into the underside of "he-story." I held her hand and cried.

Marriage and Motherhood

These are the stories of two women. One had the privilege of being a "legitimate" wife and mother but continuously wondered about the meaning of marriage. She had the safety of assured food, clothing, and shelter because she was a legitimate wife, but she also had to accept her husband's affair—also "legitimate" —because she was barren. She wanted freedom badly, but she could not go beyond the rules of Korean society.

The other woman was denied the privilege of being a legitimate wife and mother because she was not officially married to my father. This "illegitimacy" put her on the underside of history. She became a "no-name" woman, who was nearly erased from my family history. Even though she was productive, she was unable to claim her right and space as mother of the child to whom she had given life. She was threatened continuously by poverty because she did not have a legitimate husband, whose duty, according to Korean tradition, would have been to take care of his wife.

My mothers hated each other. The one who raised me resented the one who gave birth to me because she thought this woman took her husband's love away. She might better have hated her husband, but she could not; he was the one who gave her security within the structure of society. All her anger and frustration were projected onto my birth mother, the safest target to attack. For her part, my birth mother hated the mother who raised me, because she took her baby and thus became the "legitimate" mother of her child. And of course my birth mother missed me even more because the mother who raised me did not allow her to see me.

Both mothers loved their child. I really believe the mother who raised me loved me as a birth mother would have. In many ways, she totally devoted herself to me, always being there when I needed her. I still remember vividly the way she treated me, taking me everywhere she went, decorating my hair with many colorful ribbons. She often told me I was the most beautiful girl in the world, even though I was not a pretty girl at all in the ordinary sense.

When I prepared for the junior high school and senior high school entrance exams, she brought warm lunches, freshly cooked, to my school every day in order to encourage my studies. My success in school was very important to her. Once I was almost forced to drop out of college because I could not afford the tuition. At that time my father was bankrupt. We had moved to a very poor neighborhood and hardly had enough money to cover everyday expenses. I decided to give up my studies, but she would not let me. She promised to borrow some money from her close friends. On the day she was to bring the money, I sat in the registrar's office, waiting for her. Hours passed, but she did not come. I almost gave up. Then, near closing time, I saw her: my elderly mother running to the registrar's office in my college. She was sweating. I could see she was exhausted, but also relieved. Very gently, she placed the money in my hand. I broke into tears. Sobbing, I asked her, "Mother, where did you get this money? I know you have been worried about buying even the basic things." Her eyes filled with tears too. "Don't worry about that. God provided the money. You just study hard." I loved her from the deepest part of my heart. Even though I was confused by her ambivalent remarks concerning marriage and femininity, she provided me with the space I needed to explore my own daring ideas. In the ways that matter, I was her "own" child.

My birth mother loved me too. She wanted me to be the legitimate child of a good family. She did not want to ruin my social image, to make me subject to the scornful strictures that Confucian culture in the Korean tradition sets for those born outside of marriage. That was why she spent thirty years following my life from the shadows. She showed her love for me by waiting and erasing herself totally from my personal history. She told me how much she wanted to come for my college graduation and marriage ceremony. I was *her* "own" child too.

When I met my birth mother in Korea last summer, she talked about my late mother with both anger and gratitude. She was angry because my late mother despised her, yet she was thankful that I had been raised to be a healthy and strong woman.

Both my mothers were victims of a male-defined family system. My father benefited from both women. He received everyday nurturing from my late mother and a child from my birth mother. Since a child is necessary to continue a man's family lineage in Korean culture, he did not feel any social pressure against having a relationship with another woman outside of wedlock. It seemed little more than the natural order of things. But both of my mothers suffered from this social system. For them, it was not a small thing.

The only person who could bring about reconciliation between these two women was their child. Their child was the only connecting factor that could ease the bitterness between them. The love they felt for me enabled them to accept each other in spite of the chasm between them, a chasm caused by the action of a man who held so much power over them.

These are the stories, then, of two mothers who shared a child, the lives of three women bound together by love and embittered by a tradition that honors only men.

Choosing Life: My Mothers' Spirituality

Sometimes I wonder how my mothers could sustain their sanity. My late mother struggled with the burden of being a noble woman within a strenuous marriage that did not acknowledge her humanity, and my birth mother struggled to retain her dignity in the context of continuous poverty and social ostracism. As I now reflect on both mothers' histories, I realize that they used all the life-giving resources they could find around them in order to keep their lives going.

My late mother was officially a Christian. She was a member of a big church in Seoul, where she participated in a strong women's mission group. She played the role of a nice Christian lady in that church. The mission group program gave her an opportunity to express herself in a public area, providing a legitimate excuse to go out of the house. Through that program she found her self-worth as a "public" person.

However, her Christian faith was not dogmatic. She changed Christian doctrine to suit her own convenience. For example, she had a very interesting view of our ancestor spirit and developed her own religious system. Since my father was a Confucianist, my mother's duty as his wife was to prepare big feast meals for ancestor worship two or three times a month, despite the fact that many Christian churches in Korea still taught that ancestor worship contradicted the Christian faith. One day when I was six years old, one of my friends told me something she had learned in Sunday school: "You will go to hell if you continue to worship your ancestors!" This was a real shock to me, because I wanted to go to heaven. So on the next ancestor worship day, I asked my mother about the relationship between the Christian God and my ancestors. My mother answered that my ancestors were secretaries of Jesus Christ, who was a god to my mother. "Because Jesus Christ is so busy in heaven," she said, "he can't take care of every detail of our lives. That's why Jesus Christ uses our ancestors as his secretaries to get things done." My mother's answer relieved me of the fear of going to hell.

Mother seemed to have created a peace for herself between Christian faith and Confucian practice. Both figured prominently in her religious life. She also drew spiritual strength from other strains of traditional Korean religiosity. For example, she often went to female fortune-tellers[5] when she really had a life crisis. She did not go to see Christian ministers[6]—males—to solve her personal problems, even though she was officially a Christian.

My mother also went to a Buddhist temple from time to time, whenever she wanted to meet her women friends and play or dance with them. Korean Buddhism did not prohibit women from drinking, smoking, or dancing during Buddhist festivals—very different from the teaching of Christian missionaries.[7] When Buddha's birthday came, she went to the temple and celebrated with her women friends, drinking and dancing. Some orthodox Christians would say my mother was a heretic because she mixed religions and did not know the real essence of Christianity. Maybe she did not know what was orthodoxy and what was heresy, but she *did* know which things offered life-giving power. And she grasped them with both hands.

My birth mother went through a spiritual journey similar to my late mother's, even though she was extremely underprivileged by comparison. She said she was a Buddhist when she was young, and she had two dreams about my arrival into the world while she was pregnant.

In her first dream, she was inside the temple, holding me piggyback while bowing down to the Buddha. When she finished her bow, the big bell suspended at the temple ceiling began to ring. She immediately knew that my arrival was Buddha's blessing. In a second dream, she saw my father sitting on a small pagoda on Mudeng Mountain in Kwang-Ju.[8] He was wearing a rainbow outfit. Then an amazing thing happened. When she approached my father, Mudeng Mountain suddenly changed to salt. It became Salt Mountain. Salt is a positive symbol in the Korean shamanistic tradition.[9] Korean people believe that salt has the power to exorcise evil spirits. My birth mother received an affirmation of her pregnancy from the Buddha and indigenous Korean spirits. We Koreans call dreams that are connected with a pregnancy *tae-mong*[10]—dreams that show the future of the baby.

My birth mother believed in her dreams. Even though Korean society did not approve of her pregnancy, she knew that the baby came through Buddha's compassion and protection from evil spirits. I was so grateful to her for remembering the details of her *tae-mong.* I felt connected to the ocean of Asian traditions and to the revolutionary spirit of Kwang-

Ju, a small city that has been the city of freedom
fighters in Korean tradition. She said I was born there;
I did not know that. My parents had changed my
birthplace on the official governmental records in
order to hide my real origin.

My birth mother also visited fortune-tellers in
order to check on my well-being. They told her that I
would be a great scholar, and she believed them. She
said to me she *knew* that I would be very good at
school and finally would actually become a scholar.
There were no doubts in her mind.

Now she is a deacon in a pentecostal church in
Korea. I know the church very well. I hated that
church so much as a theological student; I used to
think it was dispensing otherworldly, ahistorical religious opium to the people. But after hearing my birth
mother's painful life story, I came to understand why
she chose that church. Maybe that church was the only
place where she felt comfortable, where her spirit was
lifted out of this painful world and given a place to
dream. This kind of religion can easily become an
opiate for people who have no options, no routes out
of their personal impasses.[11] Opium is like a magician,
for those who have no access to change; it enables
them to endure intolerable pain.

My two mothers mixed and matched all the spiritual resources they found around them and established
their own comfortable religious cosmos in their
hearts. Their center of spirituality was not Jesus,
Buddha, Confucius, or any of the various fortune-tellers. All these religious personalities and spirits helped
my mothers in various stages of their life journeys, but
none dominated their inner life. The real center for
their spirituality was life itself. They consciously and
unconsciously—mostly the latter—selected the life-
giving aspects of each religion and rejected the
death-giving ones. As Alice Walker said of her great-

grandmother's spirituality, my mothers "knew, even without 'knowing' it."[12] It was a matter of the epistemology of the body. Maybe their conscious selves could not catch up with what their body said because their conscious selves were not ready for the "new paradigm." Orthodoxy and heresy debates were meaningless to them, since the words themselves were unfamiliar. Most Korean women of my mothers' age could not go beyond a primary-school education. Their fathers did not send them to school. Higher education was for boys. Boys, therefore, learned how to fight against heresies, how to safeguard their narrow, privileged circles for orthodoxy. Girls did not learn the fancy words in their primary schools.

My mothers made "chemical changes" in traditional religions by infusing them with the liberative thrusts of already existing religions. Since women were excluded from the public process of determining the meaning of religion, they were free to carve out a religion on their own, without the constraints of orthodoxy. Their "imposed freedom" allowed them to develop in private a religious organic whole that enabled them to survive and liberated them in the midst of their struggle for full humanity. I want to name my mothers' distinctive spirituality as "survival-liberation-centered syncretism." The heart of their spirituality was the life power that sustained and liberated them. "Life-giving power" is the final criterion by which the validity of any religion is judged.

Inheriting My Mothers' Gardens Through Naked Dancing and Dreaming

Inheriting my mothers' gardens is a dangerous business because I inherited not only their flowers and fruits but also their insects. If I am not a good gardener, the insects will destroy my mothers' gardens. I have to look very closely at the flowers and fruits in order to pick out the insects.

I found some insects in my late mother's garden. They may be called classism, the caste system, and cultural imperialism. Since her husband had money and she was his first and only legitimate wife, my mother used her privilege against another woman, my birth mother. Still, my late mother wanted to get out of her suffocating Korean housewife's role. The problem was that she could not find many channels for her liberation.

Under the patriarchal system, which is defined by the interests of men only, women are separated among themselves according to men's needs. Because women are not the subject of their destiny and relationships but are the object of men's desire and pleasure, women are not raised to make active life-affirming relationships with other women. They are trained only to develop intimate relationships with men, and then only at the men's convenience. Under this patriarchal system, women cannot love each other. They have to be competitive and become enemies to each other because their human worth can only be affirmed by men. In my mothers' hatred for each other, I can see the most dangerous insect: patriarchy.

My late mother thought about the Western world as a model for the liberated world; she judged it by what she saw in the movies and magazines. She knew Western men opened doors for women and gave flowers to them and said "Ladies first." Therefore, my late mother assumed that Western men respected women. That was why she told me to marry one. Oh, dear Mom, I'll tell you: Even in the Western world, women are not respected and understood as you thought.

I am glad my father went bankrupt when I was eleven years old. We became very poor after that, and I learned how the majority of Korean people lived. Through the experience of poverty after my father's bankruptcy, I could see the class privilege of our family and the role we played in Korean society. This experience prepared me for the student movement and Minjung theology and finally enabled me to welcome my birth mother without feeling ashamed of her.[13]

In my birth mother's garden, I can find some insects too. Her internalized defeat took away all her power for fighting even before she started her battle against my late parents. She could not fight in this world; her consciousness told her so. She retreated to her own interior mental world, had bitter fighting there, and became mentally disordered. Mom, I am not going to run away into my inner world. I'll fight in this world, in this history, to claim my land and my power!

However, in spite of all these insects, I love my mothers' gardens. In view of the legacies of these gardens, the fruits and insects, what does it mean for me to be a theologian? It means that I must use the fruits they bequeathed to me to help create a perspective on religion that is liberating for women, a perspective that will enable us to claim our life-giving power. No longer will I accept a male-dominated religion or society but will fight until freedom comes for all women. My understanding of God is not primarily defined by the doctrines and ritualistic practices of Christian churches, Buddhist temples, or any other religion. God is found in the life experiences of poor people, the majority of them women and children, and She is giving them power not only to survive amid wretched conditions but also to overcome those conditions. The beauty of the flowers in my mothers' gardens makes me cry with joy; the bittersweetness of their fruits makes me refreshed and nourished.

Dear Moms!

Today is a beautiful day. I invite both of you to my garden. My garden is not fancy, but I am growing some strong, healthy flowers, vegetables, and fruit trees. I named them Eve, Mother of All; Mary, Mother of Jesus; Kwan-In, goddess of compassion; Pārvatī, goddess of cosmic dance; Sarah; Hagar; Du-Ran;[14] Kwang-Myung;[15] and many other women I like.

Here you can dance the naked dance again. I'll join you this time, not crying but laughing. Mary will sing the Magnificat for your dance. Sarah and Hagar will teach you the circle dance. They're a great team. You'll like them.

You would be surprised if you knew how similar your life experiences are to theirs. Pārvatī is a great dancer too. We'll have a spirit-lifting dance festival. If we become tired after joyful dancing, we can take a rest under Eve's apple tree. We can share her apples when we become hungry. Then we can take a nice nap under Kwan-In's Boddi tree. She'll lead us to a fantastic dream world. You'll meet many wise people in your dream.

How does it sound? Exciting, isn't it? Next year, I want to invite many other sisters from various parts of the world to my garden. We'll have a great time together.

Then, maybe next-next-next year, when my plants and trees become stronger, I will invite my fathers and brothers too, if they promise not to play war games in my garden. Then we'll have a family reunion.

Moms, thank you! I am so glad you taught me how to be a gardener. I am so proud of both of you.

Shalom!

> Much love,
> Your daughter, *Hyun Kyung*

27 September 1987

어머니

회색 빛 뉴욕의 추운 거리를 걸으며 어머니를 생각합니다. 세찬 바람이 뼈 속 까지 스며드는 이 겨울, 당신의 따뜻한 품이 더욱 그립습니다. 언제나 "어머니"로만 여겨졌던 당신이 이제는 비로소 한 여성으로, 한 인간으로 느껴집니다. 이제는 당신과 만나 밤을 새며 여자로서 느끼는 저의 기쁨과 보람, 분함과 억울함 그리고 황홀함을 어머니께 다 이야기 할 수 있을 것 같은데, 당신의 말씀을 웃으며 울며 들을 수 있을 것 같은데, 당신은 이 세상을 떠나셨군요. 공부한다고 이국 땅에 있으면서 어머니의 임종도 지켜보지 못한 것이 응어리져 가슴에 남아있습니다.

어머니가 돌아가신 후, 여성신학을 공부하면서 당신을 많이 생각했었습니다. 남성 중심의 문화에 의해 지워졌던 여성들의 삶의 역사를 들춰 내면서, 제가 이해할 수 없었던 당신의 행동과 말씀들이 하나 하나 이해되기 시작했습니다. 어머니, 기억하세요? 25년 전 여름, 어머니와 저와 동이 경상도 두메 산골의 어머니 친정 집을 방문하던 때, 당신이 옷을 벗으시고 인적 없는 숲속에서 노래하며 춤 추시던 일을요. 그 때 저는 비록 7 살이었지만 당신같은 어머니를 둔 것이 창피 하여 소리 지르며 울었습니다. 그 때 당신의 모습은 제게는 잊어버리고만 싶었던 어머니의 모습이었습니다. 그러나 세월이 지나 제가 성혼이 넘고 보니, 그리고 어머니를 한 여성으로 한 인간으로 이해 하게 되니, 어머니의 그 모습이 사랑스럽고 자랑스럽습니다. 이제는 왜 어머니가 숲 속에서 불을 뿜듯 춤을 추셨는지 이해 할 수 있을 것 같습니다. 특히 군래의 사촌 언니로 부터 제 출생에 관련된 비밀을 듣고서, 아버지가 딴 여성에게서 낳아 온 저를 키우셨던, 임신할 수 없어 여자 취급도 못 받고 살아 오신 어머니의 삶이 가슴 아프게 다가 옵니다.

어머니의 발가벗은 춤은 애기를 놓아야만 여자고, 남편이 외도를 하건 구박을 하건 한 남자 만은 죽을 때 까지 섬겨야한다는 남성들이 만들어 놓은 종교, 문화, 제도 속에서, 속으로만 속으로만 분과 한을 쌓고 살으셨던 어머니와 많은 한국 여성들의 자유와 해방을 향한 몸부림 이었습니다. 이제는 저도 어머니와 함께 그 춤을 출 수 있을 것 같습니다. 가부장적 문화가 우리 여성 들에게 입혀 놓은 그 거짓의 옷을 벗고, 발가 벗은 몸으로 분을 뿜어 내며, 한을 풀어 내며 어머니와 함께 명실

덩실, 해방춤을 추고 싶습니다. 그 춤의 열기 속에서 거짓 제도, 거짓 문화, 거짓 종교가 타 버리고, 새질서, 새 문화, 새 하나님 이해가 탄생할 것을 저는 믿습니다.

어머니, 어머니가 그렇게 질투하시고 미워하시되 저를 낳아주신 어머니를 천국에 만났습니다. 그 어머니도 당신만큼 강하고 아름다우신 분이더군요. 정식으로 아버지와 결혼도 못하시고 "씨받이"로 저를 낳아 어머니께 빼앗기신 후 눈물도 많이 흘리셨고 가슴도 많이 찢기셨더군요. 정식 남편없이 아기를 낳은 여자가 한국 사회에서 겪어야만 했던 모든 수모를 다 받으시고도, 가난하지만 꿋꿋하게 고통을 이기면서 살아오신 그 분을 이제는 어머니도 사랑하실 수 있으리라고 믿습니다. 비록, 이 세상에서는 당신들 두 분이 남성들에 의해 규정되었던 제도 속에서 서로를 "또"으로 미워하셨지만, 앞으로의 만남에서는 이 생에서 겪었던 강요된 아픔과 "한" 때문에 서로를 터울, 더 이해하고 사랑하실 수 있는 "자매"가 되실 것을 기도해 봅니다. 이제는 우리 세 모녀가, 그리고 "한" 많은 한국 여성들이 우주를 뒤흔드는 춤을 출 시간이 돌아왔습니다. 해방의 춤, 자유의 춤, 정의의 춤, 평화의 춤, 화해의 춤을 출 시간이 말입니다.

어머니, 이제 당신의 딸의 세대는 더 이상 역사의 그늘 속에서 눈물 흘리며 한숨 짓는 역사의 희생자로나 가야바빠 새역사를 만드는, 새 천지를 만드는 역사의 주체로서 짓밟히고 상처 투성이인 우리 민족의 아픔을, 분단의 아픔을 온 몸으로 느끼며 우리를 노예화 하는 모든 악의 세력과 싸울 것입니다. 당신들 께서 저희를 낳으시고 키우시며 생명을 주신 것 같이, 어머니의 딸들도 이 땅위에 새역사를 낳고 키우며 우리 민족에게 생명을 주려 합니다. 춤추며 싸우는 당신들의 딸들을 지켜 봐 주세요.

어머니! 큰 춤사위를 휘두르며, 지축을 흔드는 울림을 하며, 덩실덩실, 엉덩이를 흔들흔들, 어깨를 으쓱으쓱, 멋드러지게, 신명나게 저와함께 그 해방춤을 지금 다시 추지 않으시렵니까요?

" 여성 ～～ 해방 ～～ 신천지 ! "
덩 따끼 덩 딱 ! 더덩 따끼 덩 딱 ! 얼쑤 !

· · · · · · · · · · · · · ·

1988 . 1 . 25
당신의 딸, 현경 올림

PART II
Clearing
Our Space

4

Surviving the Blight

Katie Geneva Cannon

*And when we (to use Alice Walker's lovely phrase) go in
search of our mothers' gardens, it's not really to learn who
trampled on them or how or even why—we usually know that
already. Rather, it's to learn what our mothers planted there,
what they thought as they sowed, and how they survived the
blighting of so many fruits.*—Sherley Anne Williams[1]

I am most aware of the rich lore I inherited from my
mother's garden in Kannapolis, North Carolina. I
recall particularly the stories shared during devastating thunderstorms. Whenever there were gusty winds
and heavy rain accompanied by lightning and thunder, the Cannon household became—and still becomes—a folklore sanctuary. We turn off all the
lights, unplug electrical appliances, and leave the sup-
per dishes sitting in the kitchen sink. When the whole
family is seated strategically around the kerosene
lantern, my mother, Corine Lytle Cannon, moves into
her role as creative storyteller.[2]

My mother's style is to reminisce around a stock of
historical images, themes, and cultural expressions
that tell the story of the origin of Black people in
America. Much of what she recounts is based on
testimony shared across generations that her father,
Emmanuel Clayton Lytle, born August 21, 1865, was
the only free child in his family. My grandfather's
parents, siblings, and all others who preceded him
were born into slavery. One of our favorite family

legends centers around his mother, my maternal great-grandmother, Mary Nance Lytle, born in 1832. When freedom finally came, Grandma Mary walked hundreds of miles, from plantation to plantation, looking for the children who had been taken from her and sold as slaves. With only instinct to guide her, Grandma Mary persisted until she found all her children and brought the family back together.

As direct descendants of African-American slaves, my family understands such tales as the indispensable source of Black people's historical confidence and spiritual persistence despite all oppression. My mother's keen memory and her extraordinary artistic sense enable her to pass on eyewitness accounts from freed relatives to succeeding generations. These narratives are the soil where my inheritance from my mother's garden grew.

Historical Context

As a student of slave narratives, seeking the interior garden of Afro-American culture, I discovered unmistakable evidence that racial slavery in the United States was the cruelest of institutions. The unmitigated severity of slavery was based on the assumed principle of human chattelhood. As early as 1660, it was decreed that henceforth all Africans—and only Africans and their descendants—entering the Colonies would be subjected to an entire institutional framework that required them to be treated as objects, as possessions, rather than as human beings. The principle of chattelhood enabled the inner dynamics of racial slavery to expand until it penetrated the basic institutional and ideological underpinnings of the entire normative order of society.

Acquisition of Slaves

The "middle passage," the transoceanic travel of captive and enslaved Africans, has been described as the most traumatizing mass human migration in modern history. Over a period of nearly four centuries, somewhere between 9 million and 50 million people from central and western areas of Africa were seized, loaded on ships, and transported to the Americas. Each year slavers systematically hunted tens of thousands of African women, men, and children, chained them in coffles, and packed them in barracoons. People of different tribes, languages, and cultures were driven along in caravans, placed in the dungeons of slave castles or corral-like stock pens, and branded with the slave company's mark. Then they were shackled and crammed into the poorly ventilated holds of small ships, with their faces pressed against the backs of those lying in front of them. The treatment was so harsh that one out of every eight Africans died en route. So much wretchedness was never condensed in so little room as in the slave ships.

Status of Slaves

The status of chattel—mere property—was permanent, hereditary, and strictly racial. African and African-American women, men, and children were reduced to the condition of livestock and their value was calculated in real estate terms. Of all western slaveholding areas, it was in the United States that slaves were defined most completely as sources of capital accumulation and commodities. All Afro-Americans (Blacks) were presumed to be slaves unless they could establish that they had been legally freed. The legalization of chattel slavery meant that the overwhelming majority of Blacks lived permanently in subhuman status. No objective circumstance— education, skill, dress, or bearing—could modify this fundamentally racist arrangement. This mode of racial domination meant that as chattel slaves none of my ancestors were human beings legally, culturally, socially, or politically. They had no socially recognized personhood. Their status in U.S. society was literally as things. The institution of slavery and its corollaries, white supremacy and racial bigotry, excluded Black people from every normal human consideration.

Afro-Americans faced many assaults, both cultural and physical. Like domestic animals, they were literally called "stock." Their children were anticipated as "increase." My Black foremothers were referred to as "brood sows and breeders." My Black forefathers, when sold, were described, as were horses, as either "sound or unsound." At slave auctions, Black people were stripped naked, exposed to public view, and dehumanized with pokes, probes, and crude physical examinations. Often, traders made slaves run, leap, and perform acts of agility to demonstrate their "value" as chattel.

Contemporary assessments of racial slavery cannot afford to ignore this history of the virtually unlimited power of white slaveholders. The submission required of slaves was unbounded. Armed with absolute dominion over the slave, the master's power extended to every dimension, including life and death. Slaveholders had the power to kill slaves with impunity. If a slave was injured or killed by someone else, the master could claim compensation comparable to damages due when an animal was harmed. A slave suffering from such a wrong was not considered the injured party. The slaveholder was considered to be the sufferer, damaged because of the loss of the slave's labor. The death of a slave required neither official investigation nor report, any more than did the death of cattle. Non-Blacks on the American scene portrayed Black slaves to be dumb, stupid, or contented, capable of doglike devotion, wanting in basic human qualities. They used such caricatures to convince themselves that the human beings whom they violated, degraded, and humiliated or whose well-being they did not protect were unworthy of anything better.

Conditions of Slavery

Classified as pieces of movable property, devoid of the minimum human rights society conferred on others, my great-grandparents could neither own property nor make contracts. As slaves, they were not permitted to buy or sell anything at all except as their masters' agents. They could not give or receive gifts. They could not travel without a pass. Afro-Americans had no security and no protection against insults and deliberate injuries inflicted on them. There was no one to hear their complaints of ill-treatment, no power of appeal, no redress whatever. In essence, Black women, men, and children were denied all the conventionalized prerogatives of the human condition defined by the American culture.

Forced into the precise and irrevocable category of perpetual servitude *durante vita,* for all generations, Black people could not be legally married. Without the legal status of marriage, the union of a female slave and a male slave was considered as "cohabitation," which was tolerated but might be terminated at will by slaveholders. White people differentiated between the basic rights and patterns of the family life they claimed for themselves as a "democratic" nation and those they deemed just treatment for their human merchandise.

One former slave recalled:

> My pa b'longin' to one man and my mammy b'longin to another, four or five miles apart, caused some confusion, mix-up, and heartaches. My pa have to git a pass to come to see my mammy. He come some-

times without de pass. Patrollers catch him way up de chimney hidin' one night; they stripped him right befo' mammy and give him thirty-nine lashes, wid her cryin' and a hollerin' louder than he did.[3]

Slaves were constantly being robbed of familiar social ties in order that slaveholders could maximize their profits. All of the slave's relationships existed under the shadowy but imminent threat of permanent separation. Black people lived in constant fear and regularly had to endure the reality of having their husbands, wives, and children sold away from them under conditions that made it unlikely that they would ever see one another again. Relationships between both blood kin and friends were broken up by the interstate migration of slave labor. Slaveholders were at liberty to give, sell, or bequeath African Americans to other persons.

A slave owner who broke up a family was not heartless by his lights. The kindliest of masters saw nothing wrong in giving a slave child to his son or daughter when they married. An economically pressed planter might regret that husbands and wives would be separated if he moved to the Southwest, but what could he do? Sometimes debts mounted and slaves were seized by the sheriff or owners died and estates were divided.[4]

Countless slave families were forcibly disrupted.

Exploitation of Slave Workers

Be it in the Piedmont section, tidewater Virginia, the rice districts of South Carolina, or the lower Mississippi Valley, stories abound concerning my ancestors' lot, memories of stripes and torture. Their labor was coerced without wages, extorted by brute force. Slaveholders inflicted on slaves any severity they deemed necessary to make slaves perform required tasks and meted out any sort or degree of punishment for failure to work as expected or for otherwise incurring their displeasure.

Answerable with their bodies for all offenses, slaves were beaten with horse whips, cow straps, and a variety of blunt weapons. They suffered from scalding, burning, rape, and castration, sometimes dying from such inflictions. The great cruelty exhibited toward slaves resulted in instances of gouged-out eyes, slit tongues, and dismembered limbs. Sometimes slaves were physically marked by brands or tattoos or by wooden yokes or iron collars with long extended spokes. The callous and brutal system of slavery required a considerable number of slaves to wear chains, not only in the field during working hours but also at night in their living quarters. Eli Coleman, born a slave in 1846, recalled:

> Massa whooped a slave if he got stubborn or lazy. He whooped one so hard that the slave said he'd kill him. So Massa done put a chain round his legs, so he jes' hardly walk, and he has to work in the fields that way. At night he put 'nother chain round his neck and fastened it to a tree.[5]

The stark fact is that even while slaves lived under differing degrees of harshness, all slaves served under continuous duress.

> A handsome mulatto woman, about 18 or 20 years of age, whose independent spirit could not brook the degradation of slavery, was in the habit of running away; for this offence she had been repeatedly sent by her master and mistress to be whipped by the keeper of the Charleston workhouse. This had been done with such inhuman severity, as to lacerate her back in a most shocking manner; a finger could not be laid between the cuts. But the love of liberty was too strong

to be annihilated by torture; and as a last resort, she was whipped at several different times, and kept a close prisoner. A heavy iron collar, with three prongs projecting from it, was placed around her neck, and a strong and sound front tooth was extracted, to serve as a mark to describe her, in case of escape.[6]

The atrocious mutilation, too often practiced, was deeply rooted in and closely bound up with the whole existing system of chattelhood. The forms of permitted coercion effected a more complete dehumanization of slaves than had other institutional forms of slavery in earlier societies. Never before U.S. chattel slavery was a people so systematically deprived of their human rights and submerged in abject misery. The intent was to crush the spirit and will in order to transform an entire race of people, their lives and their labor, into basic commodities of production and reproduction. White supremacists in the antebellum South believed that such systematic terrorism was absolutely necessary for the continuance of their highly prized way of life and of the economic organization, social relations, and political conditions necessary to it.

Even though the customary methods of enslavement were harsh and even ferocious, Black people worked in every branch of colonial trade and commerce. In addition to the gang labor on cotton, rice, tobacco, and sugarcane plantations, Black women and men worked as cooks, waiters, nurses, carpenters, masons, valets, gardeners, weavers, shoemakers, lumberjacks, and stevedores. Enslaved workers were also forced to work in mines, extracting coal, lead, iron, and gold. They built canals and pulled barges. Slaves dug tunnels, laid rails, and staffed the railroad system. Relegated to the quarries, slaves drilled and tapped explosives, cut and polished stones, and freighted them away. Working under the lash and guarded by overseers, bondswomen regularly performed virtually the same tasks as men.

The rigor of bondage meant that chattel slaves worked always at the discretion of their owners. They could not sell their own labor. My forebears had no say as to where, for whom, or how they would work. Slaveholders dictated the nature of the work, the times for labor and rest, and the amount of work to be performed. The fruit of Black labor could not convert to financial and material gains for Black people and their families. Black people were exploited both for white people's profit and their pleasure.

Hovering over all my cultural inheritance is the devastating reality that chattel tenure excluded any sort of social recognition of Black people as thinking, religious, and moral beings. My ancestors were forbidden by stringent laws to acquire an education or obtain the means to buy their own freedom. The dominant legal and social attitude was that slaves were to be kept ignorant and living a marginal existence, fed or famished, clothed or left naked, sheltered or unsheltered as served the slaveholder. In North Carolina it was a crime to distribute any pamphlet or book, including the Bible, among slaves. Only under rigidly specified conditions could Black people take part in services of worship. Preaching the gospel, assembling together, and learning to read and write were understood simply as obstacles to the maximization of slave identity. Black people were the only people in the United States ever explicitly forbidden by law to become literate.

Cultural Inheritance

Despite the devastations of slavery, with its unremitting exercise of raw planter power and unconstrained coercion, my ancestors had the hours from nightfall to daybreak to foster, sustain, and transmit cultural mechanisms that enabled them to cope with such bondage. In spite of every form of institutional constraint, Afro-American slaves were able to create another world, a counterculture within the white-defined world, complete with their own folklore, spirituals, and religious practices. These tales, songs, and prayers are the most distinctive cultural windows through which I was taught to see the nature and range of Black people's response to the dehumanizing pressures of slavery and plantation life. Even with cultural self-expression outlawed, my ancestors never surrendered their humanity or lost sight of a vision of freedom and justice they believed to be their due. There was a critical difference between what whites tried to teach and what slaves actually learned. Against all odds, Afro-American slaves created a culture saturated with their own values and heavily laden with their dreams.

Folklore

The folktales I have heard all my life were created by the slaves throughout the antebellum South as a strategy for coping with oppression and for turning their world upside down. Operating beneath a veil of pseudo-complacency, Black women and men tapped into a profound sense of cultural cohesion, creating an expressive system of coded messages to communicate what they considered good, worthy, and meaningful. Since their survival depended on keeping their true feelings undetected in the presence of whites, Afro-Americans employed the wit, intelligence, and ingenuity of Buh Fox, Buh Rabbit, the Squinch Owl, and others to overwhelm and defeat the powerful foes, Ole Massa and his wife. An ancient Black verse describes the pro-active phenomenon of folktales in this way:

> Got one mind for white folks to see,
> Nother for what I know is me;
> He don't know, he don't know my mind.[7]

Many of the slave stories have a defensive verbal dimension so esoteric that white people miss their meanings altogether. Langston Hughes and Arna Bontemps elaborate this point in the following manner:

> While masters of slaves went to some length to get rid of tribal languages and some tribal customs, like certain practices of sorcery, they accepted the animal stories as a harmless way to ease time or entertain the master's children. That the folk tales of these Negro slaves were actually projections of personal experiences and hopes and defeats in terms of symbols appears to have gone unnoticed.[8]

Scores and scores of Blacks projected their everyday experiences and their own sensibilities onto legendary figures like High John de Conqueror, John the Trickster, and Efram as a challenge to the slave system. As C. Eric Lincoln has written:

> Every black community in the South has its multitudes of legends illustrating blacks' superior strength, sexual prowess, and moral integrity. "Mr. Charlie" is never a match for the cunning of "Ol' John." And "Miss Ann," though she is "as good a ol' white woman" as can be found anywhere, remains in the mind of the black southerner a white woman, and therefore a legitimate target for the machinations of her black servant, "Annie Mae."[9]

Living in a dialectical relationship with white supremacy, folklore was the essential medium by which the themes of freedom, resistance, and self-determination were evoked, preserved, and passed by word of mouth from generation to generation. Older slaves used folktales to reveal to their fellow slaves what they knew. As tradition bearers, they distilled this compendium of folk wisdom into instructional materials to teach younger slaves how to survive. The reappropriation of their own experiences afforded the slaves opportunities to strip away the social absurdity of chattelhood so carefully camouflaged in the dominant culture. In other words, folklore was the mask the slaves wore in order to indict slavery and to question the society in which it flourished. By objectifying their lives in folktales, Afro-American slaves were able to assert the dignity of their own persona and the invincibility of their cause.

Spirituals

Like many raconteurs, my mother always includes music in her storytelling sessions. While waiting for the ongoing storm to subside, my mother invites the family to join her in singing Afro-American spirituals. Beating time with our hands or feet, we sing about Mary weeping, Martha mourning, Peter sinking, and Thomas doubting. This genre of Black sacred music is a vital part of my family's religious tradition.

The music we listen to and sing at home is in the tradition of my ancestors, musicians who fashioned their songs from biblical lore, traditional African tunes, Protestant hymns, and the crucible of their experiences under slavery. Using their own distinct phrases, improvisational structure, polyrhythms, and call-and-response patterns, Black women and men expressed their consciousness and identity as a religious people. Some of their songs were slow drawn-out "sorrow tunes" that reflected the mood of suffering in the midst of unspeakable cruelty.

> Nobody knows de trubble I sees,
> Nobody knows but Jesus,

> Nobody knows de trubble I sees,
> Glory hallelu!

Other spirituals were liturgical shouts and jubilees, songs with reference to a future happy time. These required upbeat tempos accompanied by rhythmic clapping and holy dancing.

> Oh, my soul got happy
> When I come out the wilderness,
> Come out the wilderness,
> Come out the wilderness,
> Oh, my soul got happy
> When I come out the wilderness,
> I'm leanin' on the Lawd.

A number of spirituals were veiled protest songs used to announce secret meetings, planned escapes, and the route and risk of the freedom trail.

> Steal away, steal away,
> Steal away to Jesus!
> Steal away, steal away home,
> I ain't got long to stay here!

In essence, spirituals were the indispensable device that slaves, forbidden by slaveholders to worship or, in most cases, even to pray, used to transmit a worldview fundamentally different from and opposed to that of slaveholders. For instance, slaveholders spoke of slavery being "God ordained," while slaves sang

> O Freedom! O Freedom!
> O Freedom, I love thee!
> And before I be a slave,
> I'll be buried in my grave,
> And go home to my Lord and be free.

The spirituals express my ancestors' unflinching faith that they, too, were people of God.

As spiritual singers, slaves were not bothered by the chronological distance between the biblical era and their present. Operating on a sense of sacred time, they extended time backward so as to experience an immediate intimacy with biblical persons as faith relatives. In other words, the characters, scenes, and events from the Bible came dramatically alive in the midst of their estrangement. The trials and triumphs of Noah riding out the flood, Moses telling Pharaoh to let God's people go, Jacob wrestling all night with an angel, Daniel being delivered from the lion's den, Shadrach, Meshach and Abednego walking in the midst of flames, Joshua fighting the battle of Jericho, and Jesus praying in the Garden of Gethsemane are some of the Bible stories my foreparents committed to music as they interpreted their own experience against a wider narrative of hope and courage.

Prayer

When the rainfall's intensity and the wind's velocity drop and the lightning and the thunder recede, I know that the end of the storytelling is near. Believing that a direct personal relationship with God exists, my mother always concludes her stories with a long prayer of intercession, praise, and thanksgiving. Kneeling beside the couch, she prays for the needs of both the immediate and the extended family. She celebrates God's goodness, majesty, and mercy. She frequently enunciates thanks for the gifts of the earth and for all the blessings received. After a period of silence, my mother then provides time for every family member to bear witness to the immediate power of Jesus as "heart fixer and mind regulator."

This sacred corporate event is the direct and natural successor to the oral folklore and the religious music inherited from Afro-American slaves. Hence I grew up understanding the Black prayer tradition to be the authentic living bridge between Black people's stories,

Black people's music, and Black people's source of faith.

In the past, my ancestors met in secluded places—woods, gullies, ravines, and thickets (aptly called "hush harbors")—to pray without being detected. Adeline Hodges, born a slave in Alabama, attests to the importance of prayer:

> De slaves warn't 'lowed to go to church, but dey would whisper roun, and all meet in de woods and pray. De only time I 'members my pa was one time when I was a li'l chile, he set me on a log by him an' prayed.[10]

Sometimes they prayed while huddled behind wet quilts and rags that had been hung up in the form of a church or tabernacle, in order to prevent their words from carrying through the air. Other times they formed a circle on their knees and spoke their words into and over a vessel of water to drown out the sound. Ellen Butler, born a slave in Louisiana in 1859, witnesses to this dimension of slave religion:

> Massa never 'lowed us slaves to go to church but they have big holes in the fields they gits down in and prays. They done that way 'cause the white folks didn't want them to pray. They used to pray for freedom.[11]

The tradition of the slaves' "hush harbor" prayer meetings lives on in my parents' home. With the abiding strength of the family legends planted in our hearts, my mother invites each one of us to pray, quote scripture, lead a song, or give a testimony. Speaking under the unction and guidance of the Holy Spirit, my father, Esau Cannon, testifies about his personal experience with God. My grandmother, Rosa Lytle, "lines out" in long-metered style her favorite psalms and spirituals. The rest of the family interjects Bible verses between the singing. The last thing we utter before retiring to bed is always Grandma Rosie's prayer:

And when waste and age
and shock and strife
shall have sapped
these walls of life,
Then take this dust
that's earthly worn
and mold it
into heavenly form.

Such is my inheritance.

5

A Hispanic Garden in a Foreign Land

Ada María Isasi-Díaz

After twenty-six years of being away from my mother's garden, I returned to Cuba for a visit in January 1987. For two very special weeks, with the greatest of intentionality, I walked around *la tierra que me vio nacer* (the land that witnessed my birth), the land I have missed so very much. I tried to notice everything around me. My senses were constantly on alert, trying to imbibe every single detail, trying to sear into my heart the sights, sounds, smells of that beautiful island from which I have been gone for over half my life. The beauty of its majestic palm trees, the striking combination of green fields and white sand, the calm blue waters of the tropical sea, the immense variety of the colorful tropical plants and flowers, the exciting rhythms of its music, my Cuban sisters and brothers—no wonder Columbus said, when he landed there in 1492, "This is the most beautiful land human eyes have ever seen."

Every minute of the two weeks I was in Cuba I reminded myself I was only visiting; I was going to have to leave in a very short time. There I felt the same as I feel in the United States: a foreigner. I am caught between two worlds, neither of which is fully mine, both of which are partially mine. I do not belong in the Cuba of today; I do not belong in the States. I am repeating the history of my mother and of her mother. Grandma came to Cuba as a young woman in search of a brother who had left their home in the small village of Tineo in northern Spain and had never even written to his family. Once in Cuba she was never to go back to her native land. My mother was forty-eight when we came to live in the United States because of the political situation in Cuba. She has never gone back and now, at the age of seventy-three, has little hope of seeing Cuba again.

As a foreigner in an alien land, I have not inherited a garden from my mother but rather a bunch of cuttings. Beautiful but rootless flowering plants—that is my inheritance. Rooting and replanting them requires extra work on the part of the gardener; it requires much believing in myself to make my life flourish away from the tropical sun of Cuba. Some of the flowers I have inherited from my mother help me to deal with this situation; others at times can hinder me.

One of my ongoing gardening tasks is to find a place to plant the flowers I have inherited from my mother. At the age of eighteen I was uprooted from my country. What I thought would be a hiatus turned into twenty-six years. I am beginning to suspect it might well become the rest of my life. For many different reasons I have had no choice but to try to plant my garden in the United States. But belonging to the culture of one of the "minority groups" has meant that the plants in my garden have been seen as weeds or exotica; they are either plucked up or treated as a rarity. In general they are not accepted as part of the common garden of the dominant U.S. culture.

Most people think I should not find it too difficult to adapt my flowers and my gardening style—my cultural inheritance—to a new situation. After all, culture is always changing; it is dynamic. The fact is, however, that by belonging to a minority culture within another culture, the changing dynamic of my culture becomes a nonorganic force. The changes taking place in the Hispanic culture in the United States do not start from within but are imposed from without. These inorganic changes do not enhance the culture but rather negate it. Forced changes bring not flourishing but wilting and dying. A culture forced to change by outside forces suffers violence; its values begin to deteriorate. A culture that is not valued, whether by being ignored or by being commercially exploited, is in danger of losing little by little its will to live.[1]

This is what happens to Hispanic culture in the United States. It is sacked and raped every time we are told that our children cannot learn in Spanish in school, when our customs are ridiculed, when our cultural artifacts—typical dress, music, etc.—are commercialized. The intergenerational crisis among Hispanics goes beyond the usual differences between youth and older people. This crisis is directly connected to the lack of importance and significance given to Hispanic culture by the dominant culture. On top of the identity crisis that all young people suffer as they search for their own worth and a way to be themselves, Hispanic youths suffer from the violence against our culture in this society. No wonder they try to hide their *abuelitas,* anglicize their names, and join the world of drugs in order to have the money they think will bring recognition. No wonder I have never been able to plant my garden successfully in this society.

Trying to Plant My Garden

In the 1960s I tried to plant my garden in the convent. The enormous value given to family and community in my culture seemed to me to be the very core of this style of life. But, at least in the time when I was there, the restrictions on personal relationships that were part of life in the convent made true community life impossible. The emotional intensity of my Cuban culture was also out of place in the convent. The very poor and oppressed of Peru, among whom I worked for three years, taught me *too much,* and I could not maintain a lifestyle in which people talked about poverty while living a privileged life. Finally, my unwillingness to repress my spontaneity and passion led me to realize that my garden could not flourish within the convent walls.

If not in the convent, as a Roman Catholic woman, where could I make bloom the flower of my commitment to the poor and the oppressed? The search led me to the feminist movement. I was born a feminist on Thanksgiving weekend, 1975, when over one thousand Roman Catholic women met to insist on the right of women to be ordained to a renewed priestly ministry in our church. Failing, as the overwhelming majority of humans do, to remember my bodily birth, I am privileged to remember every detail of this birth to the struggle for liberation. But the process of "giving birth to myself"[2] was not an all-of-a-sudden experience; in many ways the process had started years before.

I spent the early part of my life in Cuba, where I belonged to the dominant race and the middle class. Growing up in the 1950s, I did not notice the oppressive structures of sexism operative in my country. But I was always attracted to struggling along with those "who had less than I did"—as I thought of the oppressed then. As a matter of fact, it was precisely that attraction which made me come to understand my vocation to the ministry. It was that attraction which I now understand as the seed of my commitment to the struggle for liberation.

At age eighteen I entered the convent, a protected way of life that used to carry with it much prestige and privilege. Therefore, the few times I came into contact with the broader society during the first eight years of my adulthood, I was treated with deference, respect, and even reverence. My life within the convent walls was very difficult, and at the time I did not have the lenses needed to understand ethnic prejudice. I was greatly misunderstood and suffered much because of it, but I did not have a good analysis of what was happening to me and how I was being treated by the other nuns.

By 1975, therefore, the only oppression I was aware of was the one I suffer within the church simply because I am a woman. It is no surprise, then, that it was in relation to church teaching and practice that I came to understand the dynamics of oppression and joined the struggle for liberation. The 1975 Women's Ordination Conference was such an intense experience that when I emerged from the hotel where we had held the three-day conference, I realized I was perceiving the world in a different way. It took a few months before I realized what the difference was that I was seeing. My eyes had been opened to the reality of sexism. My whole life had been affected; how I saw myself and what I was to do with my life had changed radically.

The struggle against sexism in the Roman Catholic Church has been the school where I have learned about feminism, as well as the main arena in which I have carried out my struggle for liberation during the last twelve years. I rejoice in the sisterhood in whose creation I have participated and am grateful for all that I have learned from the women involved in the

Womanchurch movement. This became my home. Soon I proceeded to plant my own garden there; however, that brought conflict into the sisterhood. As long as I toiled in the garden of Anglo feminism, I was welcomed. But as I started to claim a space in the garden to plant my own flowers, the ethnic/racist prejudice prevalent in society reared its head within the Womanchurch movement.

The issue was and is power.[3] Somewhat naively I had thought that together we would decide not only how to garden but what the garden was to look like, what it would be. But the Anglo feminists, being part of the dominant culture, deal with Hispanic women —and other racial/ethnic women—differently from the way they deal with each other. They take for granted that feminism in the United States is *their* garden, and therefore they will decide what manner of work racial/ethnic women will do there.

By the time I began to experience all this, I had learned much about the dynamics of oppression and prejudice and I could understand what was going on. However, what took me totally by surprise was the inability or unwillingness of the Anglo feminists to acknowledge their prejudice. Most feminists "believe that because they are feminists, they cannot be racists." Anglo feminists, like all liberals, sooner or later, have come to the point at which they are willing to "acknowledge that racism exists, reluctantly of course, but nobody admits to being a racist."[4] While whitewashing their personal sins of racism/ethnic prejudice—pun intended—in the restful waters of guilt, they continue to control access to power within the movement. Anglo feminists need to understand that as long as they refuse to recognize that power-over is an intrinsic element of their racism/ethnic prejudice, they will continue to do violence to feminism. As a liberative praxis, feminism has to do with radically changing the patriarchal understandings of power, which are operative even in the feminist movement. Anglo feminists need to remember that, in order to undo patriarchy, we must create societies in which people can be self-defining and self-determining. To achieve that, power has to be transformed and shared.

True sharing of power leads to mutuality, and that is what we Hispanic feminists ask of Anglo feminists. It is not a matter of their allowing us to share in what they define as good. Nor is it only a matter of each one of us respecting what the other says and defending her right to say it. Mutuality asks us to give serious consideration to what the other is saying, not only to respect it but to be willing to accept it as good for all. Hispanic feminists' understandings must be included in what is normative for all feminists. Our priorities must be considered to be just as important as the priorities of the Anglo feminists. All feminists must work together on deciding the priorities for the movement. This is the only thing that will allow me to continue to believe that the feminist movement "is one of the few parties left in town where we can all come together for the larger common cause. But if we're really going to boogie, power has to be shared."[5]

One of the easiest ways to understand the structure of power in society and within the feminist movement is to look at how we both construct and express what we think. Let us, therefore, look at language. For example, the fact that the word "women" refers only to middle- and upper-strata white women shows who decides what is normative. All the rest of us, in order not to be totally invisible, have to add adjectives to the word: *poor* women, *Black* women, *Hispanic* women. *Poor* women means white, underemployed, or unemployed women. *Black* women means poor Black women; Black women who are not poor are called *educated* Black women. Women *of color* in reality refers only to Black women, with the rest of us racial/ethnic women being added on as an afterthought—if we are given any thought at all. *Salvadoran* women, *Guatemalan* women—at present they command the attention of our liberal communities. After all, what we need to help change are their countries, not the United States! *Hispanic* women refers to poor women, usually Puerto Ricans, Dominicans, Mexicans, and Mexican Americans. Then there are *Cuban* women—those middle- and upper-class women down there in Miami who vote conservative. Since heterosexuality is normative in society, that meaning is also included in the words "feminists" or "women." The "others" have to be qualified: *lesbian* women, *bisexual* women.

As these examples show, power always rests with those who define the norm. Language offers us a very important tool for understanding the power dynamics in society and in the feminist movement. It clearly points out to me, at least, where I will not be able to plant my own garden and in which gardens I will never be anything but a hired hand at the very best. The net result of all this, I believe, is an impoverishment of the feminist movement, which in turn arrests its effectiveness and contribution as a liberation movement. As long as Anglo feminists do not share power within the movement with Hispanic, Black, and other racial/ethnic women, the movement will only be capable of bringing about a liberalization of those who control and oppress. Under these circumstances, the feminist movement might moderate patriarchy but it will not do away with it.

My Mother's Bouquet

As I go about trying to find a place to plant my mother's flowers, I have to look critically at this inheritance. Some of her flowers are of immense beauty and value. The one my mother values the most stands for her faith in God. *Tener fe* for my mother is to be aware of the ongoing presence of God with her and with those she loves. Faith for her is a deep conviction that God is intrinsic to her life and takes care of her. Her faith in God translates into the common everyday practice of giving credit to God for the good things that happen to her and the family. That has made her come to see that, to a certain degree, what one believes is secondary to the kind of life one leads. In my life this translates into the centrality of orthopraxis instead of worrying about orthodoxy. It is indeed from my mother that I learned we must be about doing the work of God.

A second flower my mother has given me is the understanding *La vida es la lucha*—the struggle is life. For over half my life I thought my task was to struggle and then one day I would enjoy the fruits of my labor. This is the kind of resignation and expectation of being rewarded in the next life that the Roman Catholic Church has taught for centuries. Then I began to reflect on what my mother often tells the family: "All we need to ask of God is to have health and strength to struggle. As long as we have what we need to struggle in life, we need ask for nothing else." This understanding gives me much strength in my everyday life. It has allowed me to be realistic—to understand that, for the vast majority of women, life is an ongoing struggle. But above all it has made me realize that I can and should relish the struggle. The struggle is my life; my dedication to the struggle is one of the main driving forces in my life.

A third flower in my mother's bouquet is her deep commitment to the family. While growing up she knew only a very small portion of her family, since both of her parents had emigrated from Spain with only a few members of their families. Out of this dearth of relatives came a great need to be close to the family she birthed. My mother often says that if all of us, her children and grandchildren and other members of her family, are not with her in heaven—well, it just will not be heaven! For her there is no way to have a good time if it does not involve a major number of us. Her involvement in our lives is continuous and intense. She expects each one of us to be just as involved as she is. For her, love has to be shown with words and action.

My mother's deep understanding of and need for family has given birth to my deep commitment to community and friendship.[6] Like her, I believe that apart from community we cannot be about the work of God—which for me is the work of justice. And the measuring rod for community is how it enables and provides sustenance for friendships. But community, like family, does not just happen. It requires intense, continuous work which must be given priority in the feminist movement, especially across racial/ethnic lines. I believe the building of a new order of relationships based in mutuality is at the core of feminism. And this new order of relationship must start among ourselves as feminists. That conviction is indeed based on my mother's commitment to family.

But not all of my mother's bouquet is necessarily flowers. There are also some weeds. Often, when I disagree with my mother, she gets upset, because she thinks I do not value her way of thinking and the way she has lived. But that is not true. To see things differently, and even to think that the way my mother has acted in certain situations is not the way I would act, is in no way a judgment of her. I have a different perspective and have had very different experiences. As a matter of fact, I think the difference exists in part because what she has told me and the way she has lived have pushed me a few steps farther. I believe we must take time to explain this to our older sisters in the feminist movement. We build on what they have wrought. If we only maintain what they have built, the feminist movement will retreat instead of advancing. Our older sisters in the movement must be told time and again that if we can see farther than they do it is because we stand on their giant shoulders and capitalize on what they have accomplished.

My mother has lived all her life in the private arena of the family. She has never had to work outside her home and has lived for twenty-five years in the United States without speaking English and understanding it only in a limited way. This has led her, I believe, to a lack of understanding and a distrust of those who are different from her, be it because of class, race, sexual preference, or culture. Her lack of personal dealings with people different from herself, coupled with her own personal story of having gone beyond a severely limited economic situation, has resulted in a lack of systemic analysis. For her, people are poor because they are lazy, because they do not try hard the way her mother did to give her and her sister what they needed. My mother's greatest prejudice is against those who do not have an education. She even severely criticizes people in the middle economic strata who have not studied beyond high school.

Because I grew up surrounded by this idea that people were personally responsible for the difficulties in their lives, and because of the privilege due to race, class, and social status that I enjoyed for the first twenty-seven years of my life and as a nun, I have had to struggle to make myself understand the need for systemic analysis. Three things have helped me mightily in this endeavor. The first thing was the immersion experience I had when I lived among the very poor in Peru. I often talk about those years as an exodus experience—an experience that radically changed my life. Those three years gave me the opportunity of being reborn; they made me understand what the gospel message of justice and preferential option for the poor was all about. The second thing that has been most helpful in understanding the need for systemic analysis and has given me some tools to do it has been the opportunity for study. Courses in economics, history, ethics, and anthropology have given me the tools to understand systemic conditions that make personal liberation impossible. Third, some wonderful foremothers have taught me what solidarity is all about by the way they have lived their lives. To join the liberative praxis of the oppressed, and to have personal relationships with them, has enabled me to understand systemic oppression and to go beyond thinking, as my mother does, that persons are oppressed because they do not try hard enough to overcome the limitations of their situations.

The second weed I see in my mother's bouquet is related to the first one and has to do with an inability or unwillingness to see sexism in the private sphere and to change radically in our own personal world the way we relate and operate. As the mother of six daughters who have had to struggle in the public sphere for all their lives, my mother understands and denounces the sexism she sees us struggling against in the workplace. Though many times she feels uncomfortable about my criticism and denunciation of the sexism in the church, she can deal even with that as long as it is not very public. But when it comes to the domestic sphere, she finds it very difficult to criticize the sexist behavior she sees there. This goes beyond the sense that we all have of protecting our own. What she finds difficult is not only criticizing her family but also seeing the oppression of women in any domestic sphere. I believe that what is at work here is internalized oppression; the domestic sphere has been her world, and she has come to see what happens to women in it as our proper role.

There is no way I can communicate adequately to my mother how much I have learned in our sometimes heated discussions about this issue. I have come to understand how much I have internalized my own oppression, not only in the private sphere but also in my role in the church—which until very recently was for me mainly an extension of the family. When internalized oppression moves from the private sphere to the public one, it becomes an element of a "siege mentality."

As a Hispanic I belong to a marginalized group in this society and have had to struggle to understand and deal with the siege mentality we suffer. The need to protect ourselves against discrimination is such an integral part of our lives that we are unable or unwilling to critique ourselves. It is difficult to see criticism as constructive when we are not valued by society. Those of us who as feminists criticize sexism in the Hispanic culture are often belittled and accused of selling out to the Anglo women. But Anglo feminists call into question our integrity and praxis as Hispanic feminists when we are not willing to criticize Hispanic men and culture in public. I would like to suggest that this kind of horizontal violence is linked to both internalized oppression and the siege mentality.

The challenge that lies before me has many different facets. I must struggle to convince myself and other Hispanics that our goal has to be liberation and not participation in oppressive situations and societies. We must not give in to internalized oppression and a siege mentality. We must be willing to look at ourselves and examine our experiences in view of our liberation and continue to insist, no matter where we are, on being included in setting the norm of the feminist movement. Then I have to find renewed strength and commitment to struggle with Anglo feminists over the issue of sharing power with all feminists, unless their goal is to replace one oppressor with another. Finally, I have to challenge myself and others to understand that, as feminists, the changes we are advocating will change the world radically and that we need to begin to live out those changes so they can become a reality.[7] The only way we can move ahead is by living the reality we envision. Our preferred future as feminists will only flower if we allow it to be firmly rooted in us and among us. It is up to us to change our lives radically if we want our world to change.

I plow ahead, aware that I must not idealize what I have inherited from my mother—especially because we have been transplanted and in that process have lost some of our roots and have not always correctly reinvented them. I must be careful because as transplants we often have to defend ourselves, and that can easily distort the truth. What I have received from my mother, as well as what I have gained on my own, must be subjected to the critical lens of liberation; that is the only way I can be faithful to myself and to other Hispanic women and men. The task is not easy, but the community of my family provides for me a safety net—it gives me an immense sense of security. This is one of the main reasons why, for me, hope is guaranteed and I always see possibilities. That is why I keep trying to plant my garden. That it has been uprooted several times does not keep me from trying again. Though often it is a painful struggle, I believe the feminist struggle is the best of struggles, and this is why that struggle is my life. *¡La vida es la lucha!*

Enero de 1988

Mi querida Alexandra,

Ya tienes 19 meses y empiezas a demostrar ser una niña-mujer llena de vida y de un carácter bien fuerte. ¡Qué bueno! Espero que el mundo siga cambiando para que cuando te toque luchar en esta vida no tengas tantas dificultades como tenemos hoy en día las muje- res. Fíjate, Alex, no te deseo una vida fácil. Pe- ro sí te deseo una vida en la cual la posibili- dad de un mundo justo sea más grande de lo que es hoy día.

Eres, mi querida Alex, una mujer de muchos mundos. Tus apellidos, Surasky e Isasi, lo procla- man a los cuatro vientos. No puedo menos que de- searte que las experiencias en tu vida sean tan ricas y variadas como la sangre que corre por tus venas. Pero debes también saber que inte- grar esa variedad, esa multiplicidad de cul- turas que has heredado no es fácil. Posiblemente siempre sientas tensiones —pero no consideres eso negativo. Lo mejor de la vida es llegar a balancear sin destruir los diferentes elemen- tos presentes en nuestras vidas y en nuestro mundo.

Para mí, Alex, lo más difícil ha sido el perma- necer fiel a quien soy. Ser fiel a uno mismo a la vez que tratamos de crecer —de luchar en forma responsable por lo que creemos —eso, Alex del alma, es lo más difícil. Lo que la mayoría de la gente quiere es definirnos y controlarnos —y contra eso tenemos que luchar.

Complica todo esto grandemente el ser mujer... al igual que el hecho de que yo he tenido que venir a vivir y tú has nacido en un país que cree ser el mejor del mundo y que se considera ejemplar. Porque tienes sangre cubana y americana, judía y cristiana yo espero comprendas a edad temprana que si vemos a los demás como mejor o peor que nosotras, nunca habrá paz. Tenemos que estar dispuestas, Alex, a examinar los valores, ideas y costumbres de los demás y ver si las podemos incorporar en nuestras vidas sin dejar de ser quienes somos. Eso es lo que quiere decir el aceptar a los demás... sólo entonces dejaremos de tratar de hacer que sean como nosotras; sólo entonces dejaremos de sentirnos amenazadas por otras personas y otros países; y sólo entonces habrá justicia y paz en nuestro mundo.

Tienes que ser tu propia persona, Alex. Pero nunca creas que lo tienes que lograr sola. Siempre busca apoyo, consejo, ayuda de los que te quieren. Entre ellos estoy yo, Alex... y siempre estaré. Y como tu madrina te bendigo una y mil veces deseándote fuerzas para la lucha y un deseo insaciable de SHALOM.

Te quiere,
Ada María, ...

PART III
Cultivating
a Global Garden

6

From the Prairie to the World

Joann Nash Eakin

In her concept of "our mothers' gardens," Alice Walker has provided us with an evocative metaphoric and literal term. It is, she says, a term for a "personal account that is yet shared, in its theme and its meaning, by all of us."[1] It has become the principle around which we have organized our reflections for this book, an effort most of us have found both difficult and self-revelatory.

The Garden of the Prairie

Gardens are not just metaphoric symbols for me; they are real and necessary. Without a garden to till, even though it may be only five pots on a balcony, I am not at ease. My being-rooted-in-the-soil goes back, I believe, to the gardens I inherited from my Aunt Sadie and my Aunt Nettie, daughters of Norwegian immigrant parents, sisters of my father, wives of North Dakota wheat farmers, themselves full partners in that enterprise. Years later, and far removed from the time when the highlight of the summer was to spend a week or two on their Dakota farms with Aunt Sadie and Aunt Nettie, I am amused to realize that the satisfaction I have found in the tilling of a large vegetable garden on a California hillside is a replication of their identification with the soil. I have inherited much from these stalwart, strong, hardworking, loving, and cheerful daughters of the Norwegian immigrants who homesteaded on those prairies. My cousin Dee-Dee, also a niece of these women, and I laugh to see their energy and drive in ourselves.

Deeply rooted in my soul, the prairies of North Dakota and Minnesota are one of the gardens I have inherited. I have always considered myself a child of the prairies and yet not quite of them. The prairies have not held me. In times past I have described myself as a prairie chicken who learned to fly. In reality, a prairie chicken is an awkward bird that can hardly get off the ground and that, once in flight, does not go far. As a very young child I recall telling myself that there was an ocean to the East and one to the West. I knew, with a deep certainty, that I would get to both of them just as soon as I could. And now I have lived on the edge of both these oceans—the Atlantic and the Pacific—and have traveled across many more.

The Gardens of My Mother, Inherited and Reborn

My mother, Juanita, who was unusual for her time, graduated from Iowa State University as a landscape architect. For a few years she practiced landscape design in St. Paul, Minnesota, but after marrying my father, moving to the northern part of the state, and having five children, she never returned to her profession. My father used to tease her about the plans she kept in the piano bench. It was not until I was going through trunks in the attic after her death that I came upon blueprints of parks she had designed and newspaper clippings giving accounts of awards she had won for some of these designs. In all our years of growing up she never even kept a garden, much less designed a park. I have always been puzzled by her putting aside these interests. In part, it can be explained by the customs of the time. It was not considered proper for a woman to practice a profession after marriage. Furthermore, northern Minnesota was not a hospitable climate for gardens and parks. But she always loved nature and taught us much about botany just by talking about plants. I remember her delight and joy each spring at the return of the cedar waxwings to the honeysuckle bush just outside the living room window. I inherited her love and appreciation of natural beauty, but it was much later in my life that the fullness of my dormant inheritance sprang into bloom. While living in California, I became a passionate gardener, with my head full of landscape designs.

The Garden of Love and Security

There is another garden inherited from my mother that I consider even more significant. It is the garden where love and the joy of life flourish. It is the garden remembered even by her grandchildren, who knew her only when they were very young. "Grandma Juanie was always happy and laughing," they remember. Her life was not easy, but she was always life-affirming.

Mother grew up in a family characterized by how much everyone loved each other. My Aunt Mary, mother's only sibling, until her death last winter, was still telling and retelling stories about this childhood. Papa Beard, as we grandchildren called him, often kept one or both of the girls out of school to accompany him on trips around Iowa selling pharmaceutical supplies to drugstores. The girls loved those train trips, and to the end of their lives they cherished the memories of them and of being loved by their father. Grandma Ollie, their mother, was equally beloved. They delighted in telling how Papa Beard, when on his first trip to town, saw Grandma Ollie sipping lemonade on her front porch and announced to one and all that this was the woman he would marry. Their cousin Helen, whom I never knew until I moved to California, also had many stories to tell. Her mother, a stern-faced and serious woman, had been a Methodist missionary to the Mormons in Utah. Helen loved to escape the somber confines of her home to visit the fun-loving, joyous household of my grandparents.

In turn, my mother and father loved each other and each of the five of us. I have come to understand what a precious legacy it is to have inherited such a garden of love.

Most of my growing-up years were in small towns in Minnesota. The town that was home for all my school years was on the northern Canadian boundary waters. Its one thousand inhabitants were primarily the second and third generations of Norwegian immigrants. My father was of that stock. My mother, considered an "outlander," was of Pennsylvania Dutch descent. It is with some nostalgia that I look back upon those years. It was an unbelievably safe and loving environment, a security of life not just of our family but of the whole community. As children we had only one friend who was a child of divorce, which is not to say families did not live with tension and unhappiness. Parents just did not divorce. Another aspect of our security was that as children there was no escaping into anonymity; we were known wherever we went. Our whereabouts and activities could be reported at any time.

We grew up during the years of the Depression. We were all poor, but we children did not know it. I am sure our parents struggled with the economic and social consequences. At the end of every summer my girlfriends and I took great delight in planning our back-to-school wardrobes. We each had one new sweater and one new skirt, usually purchased from the Montgomery Ward catalog but sometimes from Mrs. Fuller's Dress Shop on Main Street. We all learned to sew and became adept at making new garments from old ones. At ten I began sewing my own clothes, and to this day I design and make much of what I wear.

I have come to understand that in this garden of love and security I have inherited much from my father. His gift was believing in me. As a teacher of women's studies in social science and psychology, I have read with interest the studies that trace the "success" of women. Many women considered successful have been the eldest child in the family and have been treated by their fathers as though they were eldest sons. That is, they were given responsibility and attention and were expected to "amount to something." All this was true for me. At the age of about six I remember my father telling me he believed I would be a philosopher. What occasioned this remark I do not recall, but I *do* remember the certainty with which I knew he was right. I cannot imagine how I knew what a philosopher was, but I seemed to.

Our secure world was shattered when, on a frosty morning in December, our father was killed when a train hit his automobile. I was fourteen, the eldest of the five. Our grief was overwhelming. Mother, although she considered returning to St. Paul to resume her career as a landscape architect, decided to stay on in our community and bring us up there. In time, our life resumed and continued much as it had been. How Mother managed, I do not know to this day. I do know how heavy her heart was and how bereft she felt.

Much as Mother loved her children, she never thought we were hers to possess or "hold on to."

Rather, she was to "let us go." She often used the image of birds preparing their young to leave the nest. This is what she understood she was doing, even though she did allow herself to envy her friends whose children stayed in the community. We all grew up and left home to go to college, and not one of the five of us ever returned to live in that small town. However, the community we knew there, the community of love and security, went with us, internalized in our knowledge and memory. We carried with us an abiding trust in people and in the goodness of life.

Many years have gone since those growing-up times, and almost every day I am aware of just how much I have inherited from those gardens of my childhood, of how much of them I have claimed as my own, and of how much they have made me who I am.

From this inheritance I have acquired what seems to be a core at the center of my being. It is a core that feels unshakable, one that "steadies the ride" through the stresses and strains that come my way. I think of this core as something dense and compact, a synthesis, a boiling down of all the basic relationships, encounters, and experiences that have shaped my person. It gathers up people of the many communities I have known and loved throughout my life. It is comforting and strengthening. It is a presence within me. I like to think of it as being a little like the company of the saints.

Theological Implications of Gardens Inherited

Four primary theological concepts seem to occur and reoccur in my own theological thinking and practice. They are love, trust, community, and the ministry of the laity. It was H. Richard Niebuhr at Yale Divinity School, a theological teacher without parallel, who first introduced me to the idea that "nontheological factors" may be the most decisive shapers of our theologies. After years of theological study and a professional career in theological pursuits, I have come to see the truth of this reality. I am often surprised to discover just how early in my life much of this shaping took place.

I have learned that to be loved is the greatest gift a parent can give a child. It is a truism, but worthy of note, that having known love one is prepared to appropriate and comprehend the reality of God's love. And having been loved, one is fit and prepared to love others.

Trust seems to be like love. If you have been trusted and have been expected to live up to that trust, this experience forms the basis of your relationship with others. Trust is the basic ground of faith; without trust, it is not possible to live in faith. This kind of trust has informed most of what I do. It has shaped my belief in people, and it has been the source of my style of teaching and of my stance toward life.

Perhaps the most encompassing tenet of my theology is the concept and reality of community. I know the church as the community of God, the community of those who know and love God and of those who manifest that love in the lives they lead. I think that in the community known as the church, people know and relate to each other in ways unknown in any other community. I would go so far as to say I believe that the community of the church is the model for all other communities. I confess that when young people— friends' children, my own stepchildren—come to me speaking of their desire for community but are alienated from the church and are not looking for community there, I find myself at a loss as to where to point them, so shaped has been my own life by the community of the church.

Community is something experienced, but community is also something understood. I have come to understand community as past history that we have appropriated as our own history. It is a history that defines who we are in the present we now inhabit. I am a child of the prairie, but I am also a child of God. I have appropriated the fact that I am a child of Sarah and Abraham, a child of God: "I will take you for my people, and I will be your God" (Ex. 6:7). I am a child of the community of the people of God. This has defined my existence ever since my family filled a pew each Sunday morning in the Congregational church of our small town. Throughout my life and ministry I have continued to identify myself as belonging to the people of God.

As I noted earlier, I have come to know community not just as the security of family and small-town life but as the community "of the saints" which I carry with me. This community is composed of friends made throughout my lifetime from many parts of the world; most of these friends identify themselves as God's children, members of the community of the faithful.

An understanding of community takes me out of the identifiable institutional church into the world. It has formed the basis of how I relate to the world. Indeed, in almost everything I do, I understand that I am engaged in forming community. I believe it is in community that we find the fullness of our being.

This understanding of community has led me to the envisioning of a global network of women in theological education. Surely the fullness of the life and work of women in theological education anywhere in the world will be enhanced by our common awareness and knowledge of one another's life and work, wherever we are. The world as community, and of women as a special, identifiable, often quite separate part of that world community, has been the gift of my involvement these past several years with the Program on Theological Education of the World Council of Churches.

Another essential ingredient in my theology is an almost lifelong commitment to the ministry of the laity. Ministry belongs to all the people of God, not just to the ordained clergy of the church. Throughout my own ministry I have retained my lay status, though theologically educated. This is a decision I made out of theological conviction. However, I am well aware that some nontheological factors no doubt influenced this decision. These factors have their roots in the social, political, and economic commitments of my Norwegian immigrant forebears, some of whom were involved in the shaping and forming of the populist movement of the nineteenth century. My fervent commitment to the presumption for democracy might be traced back to their valuing the democratic traditions of their new chosen country. This commitment to the ministry of the laity was nurtured during the days of my involvement as a university student in the Student Christian Movement and later, during my years as a campus minister. At that time, the ideas of Hendrik Kraemer on the theology of the laity were very much a part of our thinking.[2] It is significant to note that since Kraemer wrote his definitive work in 1958 there has not been another work of the same theological depth on this subject. And some may argue that the church of today has a superficial understanding of the ministry of the laity, one which sees laity as ministering to the institutional church, not to the world.

My commitment to the ministry of the laity deepened and acquired a wider range of meaning during the years I was director of the Master of Arts in Values Program at San Francisco Theological Seminary. This is an external degree program designed for the laity with an emphasis on their ministry in the world, particularly in the context of the ethical dilemmas encountered in the practice of their professional and family lives.

Most of us in the West live bifurcated lives. Our life in the church is separated from our life in the world. The result is that the convictions of Christians have little influence on the conduct of world affairs.

My concept of the ministry of the laity has been enlarged, enhanced, and reinforced by my acquaintance and experience of ministry lived out by lay people in Latin America. My primary contacts have been with the Theological Education by Extension movement, which flourishes in most of Latin America. The vitality, urgency, theological curiosity, and thirst for education of students in these theological programs, many of them lay people and more and more of them women, is like nothing we have found in the United States or Europe. Our experience in this regard is limited; we have no pegs upon which to hang this phenomenon, and therefore we have difficulty understanding it. Those studying in these Third World programs are not involved merely on an abstract level; rather, they see that these studies have everything to do with their lives in the struggle for economic, social, and political change. Their life and involvement in the church and in Theological Education by Extension programs often is the force that compels them to reflect upon their faith and to see their life situation anew. Thus they imagine new ways of living and being in their society, and these insights lead them to act in significant new ways.

Ministry Among and with Women in Theological Education

All these theological concepts—love, trust, community, ministry of the laity—have found expression in my ministry among and with women in theological education. In the late sixties and seventies I was one of the founders of what has come to be the Center for

Women and Religion of the Graduate Theological Union in Berkeley, California. Since then and up to the present moment, I have worked with communities of women in theological education and in ministry in the United States, Europe, and Latin America.

In the past twenty years much has happened to affect opportunities for women in theological education and in the ministry. It is also true that not enough has happened. It is clear to many women that fundamental changes in the structures of theological education and the churches have yet to take place.[3]

In many seminaries in the United States we know that women are 50 percent of the student body. But women still have a struggle in receiving calls to ministry, in being accepted as pastors, and in finding opportunities for larger responsibilities. There are women who, given the difficulties they have encountered in ministry in the churches, become discouraged and disillusioned and leave the established ministry. Often they develop new forms of ministry, "parachurch," alongside or outside the established church.

In many parts of the Third World, women have an enormous struggle just for the opportunity to study theology. Once engaged in theological study, a woman is often understood to be preparing to be a minister's wife, and even when she has acquired a theological degree, along with a minister husband, she is still expected to function only as the minister's wife, with no recognition of her own gifts or competence. The oppression exercised by men in the church is still profound and capable of killing the spirit of women. The situation changes only as women band together, find their common voice, and begin the struggle to challenge the status quo. It is not easy in traditions where the dominant culture of the churches is a prevailing masculine one. This male church culture is firmly in place even in those traditions where, in the

wider social and economic realm, women have important functions and roles.

Toward a Global Network of Women
in Theological Education

My involvement with women in theological education, in ministry, and in the church has continued to
evolve. The most recent form of this involvement is
the envisioning of a global network of women in
theological education, born out of the discovery of
small (and not so small) networks of women in
theological education all over the world. Few of these
networks are aware of the work, the scope, or even the
existence of many of their counterparts. All would be
encouraged, sustained, and enriched by a knowledge
of one another's work.

In the Third World, groups of women are struggling
to gain a foothold in theological education, struggling
for the right to study, struggling to fulfill their ministry, and struggling to find employment as pastors or
teachers in theological school. Everywhere I go I have
been amazed, impressed, and empowered by the
vigor, imagination, and creativity of these women's
caucuses, groups, and networks. In many parts of the
world, particularly in the Third World, it is often
difficult to find and identify these groups. In the Third
World, women are not often in the center of the life of
institutions of theological education. In many instances these women's groups live alongside, on the
margin of the established institutions, often unno-
ticed and unacknowledged. Not everyone has the
opportunity to travel to the corners of the world where
these women are, but we all have the right to know
what is happening there. My commitment to the idea
of a global network of women in theological education
is based on the simple and basic idea that we all have
much to learn from one another.

The fundamental idea of a network is that it is an exchange system: an exchange of ideas, resources, programs, work-in-progress, and people. It is also an identification of these ideas and resources. The chief function of a network is to share information, to make connections; it is a communication system. It makes available the resources of one group for the benefit of others. A network is also more than this. It is a source of inspiration and motivation. It is an empowering force. A network does not have one nucleus; it has many nuclei with connections in all directions.

The worldwide women's movement has a particular affinity and talent for networks and networking. Information and knowledge are not something women claim for themselves alone. Rather, they have a sense of responsibility about sharing what they have and an eagerness to learn from one another. To know about the ideas, programs, and publications of other women's groups often provides inspiration and gives confidence to women in their struggle to form their own communities and centers.

All over the world women in theological education —students, faculty, and administrators—are naming their identity, affirming their collectivity, developing programs and curriculum, and publishing their writings. In some countries these efforts are barely visible or only exist as a vision of what might be. In others, there are centers of women that have accumulated a history and acquired a maturity as a result of some years of existence. Women in theological education in one part of the world rarely know about developments in another; this is as true of the First World as it is of the Third. Global awareness is imperative if we are to consider ourselves members of the worldwide ecumenical movement.[4]

When asked to make a connection between and among the various forms my ministry has taken, I can only respond by saying that I trust and believe in the grace of God. I cannot say I have had a series of five-year plans—or even ten-year plans—for the development of my career. Opportunities have emerged and I have responded; one involvement has led to another. And certainly the experience of living in the context of the community of the church out of which these opportunities have emerged has been a major factor. I have moved from the prairie to the world, carrying with me in that journey all that has formed me from my growing-up days on the prairies of Minnesota and North Dakota.

7

My Mother's Garden Is a New Creation

Marta Benavides

A mi mamá y a mi gente que la formaron.

Struggling myself don't mean a whole lot, I've come to realize. Teaching others to stand and fight is the only way our struggle survives.—Ella Baker (1903–1984), Black U.S. Civil Rights activist with SNCC

I didn't want to get up. It was too early, only three in the morning. I was about five and my youngest sister was a six-month-old baby. This is the first clear memory I have of making the journey to my mother's home. El Salvador is a small country, so distances are not so far, compared with Mexico or the United States. But still, if one has to walk from one end of the capital city to the other in order to board a bus, it's a long way! And the bus is so crowded and makes so many stops. We were carrying loads—mountains, it seemed to me at the time—of books, clothes, medicines, toys. It was a heavy burden, though I saw only happiness in my mother's face, the same happiness as in the days before the trip, in spite of all the extra work. She was elated; she was going home to the high mountains where she was born and raised. The small one-room home at the *meson* where we lived, a small city building with many rooms for rent, one per family, oppressed her. Although she had planted a garden of flowers, herbs, and tomatoes in milk cans

near our room, her longing for nature was not satis-
fied.

We were three daughters at the time, and as we
walked through the city, our parents talked to us,
especially our mother. I suspect that it was not only to
keep us from complaining and to make the walk seem
shorter, but also to share their visions and values, the
way they saw life and its possibilities. I remember my
mother telling us about the beauty of each new day.
She told us to listen to the different songs with which
birds greet each new beginning. She also pointed out
the many rich colors of the sky, and the burning
orange of the rising sun. We were, she said, to start the
new day just like that, filled with beauty, rich with
expectation. She asked us to breathe the fresh air
deeply. She made us take notice of the hustle and
bustle of our people, already at work at four in the
morning. She reflected that there was no rest for the
poor: no paid vacations, no benefits, no pensions or
social security. We must always work and work hard,
she said. Many of our poorest people even had to work
as beasts of burden, carrying big heavy loads of corn,
beans, potatoes, or bananas on their backs. A large
percentage of our women, who are single heads of
households, balance on their heads big heavy baskets
of fruits, vegetables, chickens, or bread as they spend
the day peddling their goods on the streets, all the
while carrying a baby in their arms. My mother
painted these pictures vividly for us, even as we were
watching people doing exactly what she described.
Nevertheless, in spite of the work we do, we are not
beasts of burden, she said, we are people of dignity.
That is why we work so hard, because we want to have
the right to determine our lives rather than be dependent on others. We all are God's children, part of the
whole creation, and creation is sacred, part of a
holistic plan, where everybody and everything has an
important role to play. Therefore, nothing should

be wasted or mistreated, for everything is part of life.

We arrived at the bus depot, which was already bustling with activity, even at such an early hour. The bus was very crowded, but we secured seats because we were early and my father moved quickly. He took my sister and me inside the bus, and my mother handed the baby and other things to him from outside. On top of the bus were all kinds of bundles, from grains to clothes to chickens. We traveled for an hour and a half, the bus puffing and pulling, until we got to Sonsonate, where we changed buses for San Julian, a small town about an hour away. This bus was as crowded as the one before, but the landscape, no longer rich green valleys, became mountainous.

San Julian is a small old town, typical of the towns the Spaniards laid out, with the Catholic church and the municipal building surrounding a park in the central square. It is here that the municipal band plays on Sunday afternoons at the *glorieta,* a gazebo, which stands in the center. Flowers and trees flourish in the surrounding gardens, and there are decorative iron benches for people to sit on while relaxing under the old orange colonial lights. It's a miniature Mexican Alameda Park, just like *Alameda Sunday Afternoon,* the painting by famous Mexican muralist Diego Rivera. But no one was in this park; it was still early morning. People come later, in the afternoon and evening.

We went straight to the market nearby, where we bought some *café con leche*—hot coffee mixed half and half with hot milk—to drink with our French roll and cheese, while my mother looked for a truck driver to help us to continue our journey. Once the deal was made, my mother and sisters traveled with the driver in the cabin; my father and I sat on top of the bean, sugar, and rice bags piled on the bed of the truck. We climbed up and down the hills, mostly in second gear, constantly blowing the horn at each turn because the dirt road was very narrow. I ducked under tree branches to avoid them, after having lost my pretty head scarf, which stayed hanging pink on the green tree behind me.

The scenery was, and still is, awesome and full of beauty: majestic volcanoes; vegetation thick with all shades of green; poinsettias, red and tall, bordering the roads; colorful, sweet-scented morning glories climbing bushes and trees; coconuts, bananas, oranges, guavas, avocados, mangoes, and mammees; coffee trees in the shadows under the tall trees; calm creeks crossing the road; waterfalls rolling down the mountain just one arm stretch from me. There were many people coming and going. Most were barefoot; some wore *caites,* very durable sandals with tire soles. They shouted good morning and *"Vaya con Dios";* there were also plenty of oxcarts, with their heavy cargo. But what I liked best were the people riding horses, with their bundles on a second horse following behind. (On another trip, I had to ride a horse and an oxcart, for it was the rainy season, and the truck could not climb the steep clay road.)

At the *desvio*—the Y in the road—for Ishuatan, we said goodbye to the driver. Carrying our bundles, we climbed down a steep mountain. At the bottom ran a clear river, where water jumped rapidly around very large stones, which were to be our bridge. We ate lunch in the middle of the river, sitting on one of the stones. We played for a while with the fish and the crabs amid the luscious vegetation. Then we followed a *vereda,* a one-person path, between mountains amazingly planted with corn. At the beginning I was screaming, terrified, as we encountered snakes, *tepeiscuintes*—a kind of rodent—and iguanas. We saw a variety of other animals and birds. There were rabbits and Cornish hens everywhere. My mother laughed heartily and calmed me, explaining that all of them are good and delicious food. We should treat them with respect, just as Saint Francis of Assisi taught. In spite of the whole experience I was still resenting this hike and wondered what I owed God to deserve such punishment.

Finally we arrived at the top. I knew it when we got to the *portillo,* a kind of fenced entrance to the farm. With my mother, we turned to look back at the road we had just traveled. There was beauty all around us. I felt the closeness of nature. The sun was going down, and the rich orange color was in front of me again— for the second time in one day. From here I could see far away; in the distance there was a pearl shining in splendor. It was the Pacific Ocean. My mother told me that was near Farabundo Martí's hometown. (She was to tell me about Martí the next day.) There were tall beautiful trees I had never seen before, and the air had a special pleasing fragrance from the balsam tree—a kind of eucalyptus. Besides its beauty and particular fragrance, the tree has many medicinal qualities. That variety of balsam is native here. At the beginning of colonization, the Spaniards exploited the balsam, calling it *bálsamo del Perú* to confuse the pirates when they were taking it to Spain. I was to learn much more about the tree.

We went to the *rancho,* an ample wood structure with bedrooms all on one side, living room in the middle, and spacious *corredores*—big porches— surrounding the whole house, with hammocks to sit in and tables to eat from. The kitchen was outside, a separate structure, equipped with a wood-burning earth stove and a *comal* to cook the tortillas. There was a special kind of podium for the stone on which to grind the corn. In a corner were *cántaros*—clay basins —to carry and keep water from the creek. The toilet was a small shack in the woods. There were no electric lights, but there were kerosene lanterns, a battery Phillips radio, and an RCA manual record player.

We celebrated for a while. People had seen us come up the mountain and brought their children to visit, knowing my mother had come home. We children played all kinds of games on the patio. We told legends about our ancestors; many of them were ghost stories. But it gets dark quickly in the mountains, and people get up to work with the *Nixtamalero,* as we call Venus in Nahuatl, a language of the native peoples in Central America, and that is very early. Most of the children had never stayed up so late. In the mountains of El Salvador, we say that people go to bed when the chickens fly to their nests. One of the children said to me in amazement, "Look at the beautiful lanterns that Tata God has put in the skies for us tonight!" I have never forgotten that moment and that reflection. It comes back often to talk to me, as I go, in exile, in search of my people.

We got up very early the next morning. My mother and I went to the *ojo de agua,* the eye of water, where the creek is born. We bathed and filled the *cántaros* with the cold mountain water, just as she had done as a girl. Then she carried the water on her head, as is the custom. I tried to do the same with my small *porrón* and found out how heavy water is and how difficult to carry in a jug on the head. We also walked to the one-room school my mother attended; it was very basic and at least 4 kilometers—2½ miles—away. She told me of the great respect and admiration she had for her teacher. He was good, and was paid almost nothing. He taught about twenty-five boys and girls of all ages. The last time she saw him, he was dead. He and his son had joined the people's uprising in January of 1932. Farabundo Martí was the leader; he had lived not far from here. He returned from Nicaragua, where he fought on the side of General Sandino, to organize the people to obtain their rights. It was the very poor, native, barefoot people who rebelled. They were all charged with Communist conspiracy, she said, so they shot, hanged, and beheaded them. These roads were red with blood. After the *maestro* was killed, my mother did not have a school or a teacher ever again.

As we returned, we went to see the *bálsamos*. People had climbed them to make cuts in the tree bark. The cuts were covered with rags to soak up the thick sap of the tree. My mother was sad. The owners were like vampires: they only wanted to get the milk out, they had no regard for the well-being of the trees, which had started to die. With the leaves, the *pepa,* or seed, and the sap, one could make all kinds of medicines and ointments: to heal cuts, clear the skin, cure headaches and stomachaches, and beautify the hair. The leaves could be burned to keep the mosquitoes away. I learned to love the *bálsamo*. My mother, who also loves the tree, has been able to germinate the seed in exile. She has a small *bálsamo* tree with her. I know that only changing to a government that is representative of the people would bring the necessary measures to cultivate rather than exploit the *bálsamo.* The same government would care for, rather than exploit, the people: the infants, the children, the widows.

As we visited in the communities, we took toys for the children, many of whom had big bellies from parasites. My mother talked about the different herbs that could cure them; she knew the importance as well as the means of getting rid of the parasites. As we walked from hut to hut the situation repeated itself: people were very poor and malnourished. Most of them went from one *hacienda*—big coffee plantation —to another, picking coffee and doing other work necessary to the coffee harvest. The children would be left alone on the side of the road. The family would eat only rice, tortillas, and beans. Sometimes it would be tortillas with limes. When times were really hard, it would be tortillas with salt.

My mother was angry with the rich people and had

no respect for them. She said that life was sacred, and the rich who had chapels on their own *haciendas,* to which the priest would come to minister directly to them and them only, were sacrilegious. Later in my life, when I became a Protestant, my mother respected my decision. However, she did not want to participate herself, because she saw the church always taking, in one way or another, from the people. The priests and pastors were always growing in importance, but the well-being of the people was never a priority. She characterized the archbishops as always dressed with expensive embroidery, blessing the military governments that robbed the people. One particular case, that of Doña Elenita, was difficult for her to ignore. The priest took advantage of Doña Elenita's granddaughter, who was a young teenager. Through various means he was able to get her small widow's pension, leaving her emotionally and economically destroyed. My mother used to root some of her jasmine, *ruda*—a medicinal plant—and carnations for Doña Elenita to sell. Mother also gave Doña Elenita and Señora Conce, the woman who peddled vegetables and fruits in the streets, beans, rice, corn, and coffee.

I participated in all these arrangements and transactions, visiting the people who were my mothers' friends in their poor huts. Later on I became a godmother, a *comadre,* which is a secret I learned to keep from my church, which considers these Catholic rituals non-Christian. My mother's definition of spiritual was to care and act on behalf of life, to keep people alive. Religion, she said, is not sacred; people and life are sacred. So I learned the importance of spirituality, and the banality of rituals and religion that don't respond to justice.

We were also good friends with many native people, and this caused us many problems with the neighbors. One native girl, Chicu, became my mother's goddaughter and lived with us for a while because her

mother was gravely ill. There were insults and discrimination because we were also seen as low-class
Indians, or servants.

Another situation was when young teenage maids
were assaulted and raped by the husband or oldest son
in the house where they worked. They were then
kicked out of the house in the middle of the night with
nothing to take with them—not even their salary—
and accused of robbery or prostitution. My mother's
response was to take them in, and this caused us many
troubles with the neighbors. As always, my mother
took her stand and taught us the importance of being
on the side of justice.

My mother had to work very hard in all the
domestic chores. She washed by hand, cooked, ironed,
and cleaned. Yet she found time to teach herself to sew
so she could work at home and earn money to help
with expenses. She became a very good seamstress
and people looked especially for her. She took great
pleasure in making beautiful embroidery for my sisters and me. The sewing and the gardening were acts
that pleased my mother's heart, for both of them were
a way of creating. My mother also planted her gardens
because of her desire for roots and in order to build
community.

Many years have gone by, and my whole family has
had to leave El Salvador. Last year, I watched my
sister plan and plant a garden where she now lives. She
did it because she felt uprooted and needed to feel
stable in her new community. This year I have witnessed the beauty that has come forth from her
garden: the variety of colors, shapes, and designs. I
thought of my mother's tiny gardens. I now understand much more clearly; gardening is about visioning. It is about faith, hard work, patience, beauty, and
sharing. Gardening is about dreaming and futuring. It
is one of my mother's legacies to me.

My mother studied the Bible with us girls, and we

prayed together. She read to us the Prophets, Mary's song, and stories of Jesus. She demanded that our actions be consistent with God's call for justice. It was through these experiences that I started to understand that what we practice must be intentional, directed, planned, and transforming. Justice requires not just action but reflective and responsible action.

When I was about twelve years old, I became a *señorita;* that is, I started to menstruate. My parents sat down and explained to me and my sister what was happening to me and the possibilities that would come with this development. My mother encouraged me to think clearly about the future and to reflect that I was here to make a contribution for a better world. This included making El Salvador a better nation for all of us—with jobs, education, houses, and food for all the people. She said I should be careful and think carefully about marriage. But first I should go and see the world for myself and only get married once I had a degree. This was so I could defend myself and help my sisters and others. Also, if my husband mistreated me, I could kick him out of the house and take care of the family myself.

All these reflections and discussions helped my understanding of the how and why of my praxis. Everywhere I have been, I have become involved in activities to help change society to be more just. When I studied in the United States, I consciously decided to accept lower grades, though I had been an A student in El Salvador, in order to seek to learn as much as possible about U.S. society. Through working with migrant farmworkers in South Jersey, I learned with them the importance of political study and reflection. We learned that it is not social services or activism that make the difference, it is effective political activity. This means that one must understand history, study the issues, be willing to change, work in unity with others, and avoid perfectionism. I also learned that justice cannot prevail by merely studying, talking, or writing about it. With the farmworkers I also learned to present difficult subjects in very simple ways. I still do this.

Before I finished my school program, Archbishop Oscar Romero, with whom I had been corresponding, asked me to return to El Salvador to work with him as an ecumenical adviser. He was very concerned about unity and wanted us to develop concrete ecumenical programs that were supportive of the people. My mother respected Monsignor Romero very much, but when I announced my plan to work with him, both of my parents resisted. My mother told me, crying, that I was not Jesus. She meant by this that I could pay with my life for this involvement. Many people perceived that Monsignor was a marked man. I tried to persuade them differently, for family unity was very important to me. My father said I would give my mother a heart attack; my mother said the same thing about my father. They wanted me to help our people but not in this way; they wanted me to find something safer. One day we agreed to role-play. I became the peasant, my father was the oligarch, my mother portrayed the National Guard (one of the most repressive military organizations in El Salvador), and my sister guided our roles. We role-played the situation and the confrontation right up to the point when my mother, as the National Guardsman instigated by the oligarch, decided to kill me because of my demands. When they realized I understood the magnitude of my decision to work with Monsignor Romero, they stopped begging me to change my mind and began to support me.

Today I live in Mexico, working with refugees from my country and with other oppressed groups. I spend some time in El Salvador each year. I also go to the United States to meet with U.S. women—to work hard at being a real *compañera* with women of justice in this country. It is important for me to garden with others. To garden with others is an expression of solidarity; that is what being *compañeras* is all about. Gardening is visioning, dreaming, and futuring for me too. It is to envision and bring about the new earth, right here and now. But I cannot bring about the new earth by myself, because a new earth demands that we look at the universe in which we are immersed. We must see what is old and decadent and death-giving: infant mortality, unemployment, profit valued more than people, militarism, the arms race. We must look for the new we are called to bring forth; health and education for everyone, soil conservation, food with no preservatives or pesticides. We could develop a technology that is responsive to the needs of people and the laws of nature and not make whole nations dependent on transnational corporations. This technology will require much plowing and hoeing; it is hard work. It is the challenge to bring about the promise of the new creation, as described in Isaiah 65:19–22, 25 (TEV):

> There will not be weeping there, no calling for help. Babies will no longer die in infancy, and all people will live out their life span. . . . People will build houses and get to live in them—they will not be used by someone else. They will plant vineyards and enjoy the wine—it will not be drunk by others. . . . They will fully enjoy the things that they have worked for. . . . Wolves and lambs will eat together; lions will eat straw, as cattle do.

For us in the Third World, this describes and sets the measure of what true development should do. What I do locally or in my nation must be imbued with this spirit of the global call. One cannot happen without the other. And this spirit of the global call must be incorporated in all local action.

Let's look at the case of Nicaragua. For true development there, peace and justice are needed first. For Nicaragua to win against the aggression of the United States and its effort to make the country surrender its sovereignty, the Nicaraguan people must be *united*. To unite, they must own their history. They must feel the need to defend a government that provides equality of opportunities for all races and both sexes and feel that with their government they are forging a future for all. However, in order for their stand to be effective and to be achievable, Nicaragua must deal with the unjust foreign policies of the United States, which have included mining their harbors, sabotaging the Contadora process and the Arias Peace Plan, and occupying the whole country of Honduras for *contra*-revolutionary purposes. The international community must understand that it is also being subverted and sabotaged and having its sovereignty denied when their ships are threatened with destruction and their crews with death because their ships are carrying dry milk or oil to Nicaragua.

We need to educate the citizens of the United States about the need to search for effective peaceful solutions to the conflict in Central America. That is how we show our commitment to peace and justice, because effective solutions will change the power relationships of the countries in this hemisphere and in the world. We must also effectively turn the tide of the arms race and increasing militarism. In order to do that we have to change the understanding of what national security is and have a clear understanding of what is in the national interest of the people of the United States. The concept of the new earth challenges us to make sure that the interests of the majority of the people of the world are taken into account. The current U.S. policy requires Nicaragua to cry "Uncle." Since this is the case, many people in El Salvador, Mexico, the Middle East, South Africa,

the Philippines, as well as farmworkers, Blacks, Hispanics, and women, must also cry "Uncle" rather
than claim their right of self-realization and human
fulfillment. Only then can each nation work at its own
garden, interdependent with each other, making
Mary's song a possibility.

We must understand that each of us is able to have
our own garden only when we cultivate it in the
context of global interdependency and mutual respect, regardless of color, sex, religion, or national
size. This is why I say that gardening is a serious and
difficult business! It takes much study and critical
reflection as well as networking and hard work. Prayer
affords us the spiritual strength for this difficult task.
Gardening has to do with *compañerismo:* standing
beside one another; being of the same company and
commitment. That is what our struggle should be no
matter where we are. As I work in my Salvadoran
garden, I also prepare the ground and work in the
garden of all those other nations and persons striving
for liberation.

Another word for *compañerismo* is solidarity. I
stand in solidarity with the poor and oppressed as I
rejoice and defend the right for self-determination for
Nicaragua. This expresses itself concretely in day-care
centers for the babies of the market women in Nicaragua. When I affirm the trials of the military responsible for the suffering of the Mothers of the Plaza de
Mayo in Argentina, I also practice solidarity. Mutuality and solidarity is what *compañerismo, compañera,*
and *compita* is all about. That is why the people of El
Salvador chanted on the streets in 1987 the same
chants as on the day of Monsignor Romero's funeral
in 1980: *"Compañero Oscar Arnulfo Romero, presente,
ahora y siempre."* Solidarity has a dimension of being
with the other in spite of distance, time, and physical
presence. Monsignor Romero was able to capture the

heartfelt aspirations of the people of El Salvador; he died defending them, and he is present now and forever.

Our solidarity is a reflection of a God who is with us as *Compañero.* The passages of the Bible, such as those in Isaiah about the new earth, tell us that God's plan is for each and every one of us to live in justice and freedom. When God's new creation is fulfilled, we will have the real garden in which everyone can dwell as companions in peace. Since the time that Columbus got lost and claimed he had "discovered" us, we have been struggling to hold on to our gardens and the right to cultivate them. The people who came robbed us of the land we had held communally; they killed our people and destroyed our culture and records. They replaced our gardens with their profit-making crops—coffee, cotton, and sugar. They exported the fruit of our land and left us with the weeds of malnutrition and high infant mortality.

My people have rebelled not once but dozens of times and long before Castro was in Cuba or before the U.S.S.R. was established. Each time my people have been massacred. In 1932 La Gran Matanza took place in El Salvador. One eighth of the population— men, women, children, and elderly—were killed within two weeks! They said this was to save us from communism. In fact it was to keep us from planting our gardens of corn, vegetables, and beans. It was to keep their exploitive commodity crops. They massacred us in order to keep our land as their own private property. We became a garden owned by the United and Standard Fruit companies, a "banana plantation" in the backyard of the United States. Our country was viewed as "backyard"; our people were viewed as "weeds." Now things are worse. The U.S. government considers us their "front yard" and spends millions of dollars bombing Salvadoran villages and protecting those they control by resettling them in model villages just like the ones they set up in Vietnam during the 1960s.

The U.S. government does all this by ignoring what 65 percent of the American people want and by sending hundreds of millions of dollars in military aid to torture and kill those working for peace and justice in Central America. They are killing the artisans, the weavers of Guatemala, Mexico, Peru, and Brazil, with the hunger caused by the astronomical international debt. These millions of dollars rob the native people of Central America of their chance to weave their own lives and to plant their own gardens. They also rob those in the United States who are under- and unemployed, senior citizens, and poor women and children who need the tax money for their survival. There is money to militarize the skies and dump acid rain on whole nations, but then we need rock concerts to fight starvation in Africa and depend on dimes to fight degenerative diseases. Exploitation, support of the *contras,* and militarization are weeds with very deep roots. We must weed them out intentionally, tenaciously, and consistently.

The garden I inherited from my mother has become for me the whole of creation. We all need to join together to live as *compañeras* and tend the global garden. Time is of the essence. The powerful people of this world use their think-tanks to rob our people of their rights—human rights. The powerful take everything away from us by spending their time and money to figure how to keep us in the rat race; living by "the gospel according to mortgage." We must reverse this condition and make real connections between the gardens of El Salvador, Central America, and the whole world.

I am one with my nation just like the plants and flowers are one with the soil. But the soil of El

Salvador has been plundered, and there is almost nothing for us to inherit. The land, the indigenous ways of El Salvador, our language and traditions— everything is being gradually destroyed. All that we have left is ourselves and the future we forge. Our inheritance, above everything else, is our will to survive as a self-determining people. That is also the only legacy we have for our children. What a wonderful flower! No pesticide can kill the will to survive.

This hope in the future is very much part of my life as a Christian, for as Christians we are called to be partners with the Creator and the creation as we work for the fulfillment of God's new creation. To know the promise of God is to follow it as a way of life every day and in every struggle. By walking according to Jesus' commandment of love, we work to achieve a creation where such love can be shared. This way of life begins with a grounding in the reality of the world and the society in which we live. It is in this context that we try to discern God's plans and objectives and try to choose the effective ways to work for God's promise of new creation. It becomes our responsibility to know how decisions are made: decisions that affect our destinies and the quality of our daily lives. We must know who makes the decisions and what are the results. Let us watch the elected officials who enact the laws and carry them out, so that they help to bring this new garden. Our calling is to be effective political beings, if we are to be agents of our history and forgers of a new future. Thus it is not words but deeds that help us to recognize our *compañeros* and *compañeras* in legislatures, courts, government administration, and church or community action groups. We must be willing to stand up and pay the price, day in and day out. We must clarify our direction and keep on the freedom road. It does not matter how steep the road, or if at times we have to go up the *arroyo*.

All of us women in the First, Second, and Third Worlds need to be about struggles that are real and not just academic. And these gardens of struggle are linked to the powerful gardens of the United States, Europe, the Soviet Union, and Japan. In the United States the flowers that should be growing in our gardens are flowers of the Equal Rights Amendment, of grape boycotts for the United Farm Workers in their struggle against pesticides and dangerous wastes, of struggles for economic justice. The flowers we need go on and on. These also include learning about the responsibility to support the struggles of the Native American nations to keep their homelands and have their treaties, their culture, and their spirituality respected. There is the struggle for economic rights in depressed Appalachia and putting an end to strip mining which destroys the ecology; advocating rights for senior citizens and the civil rights of our Black brothers and sisters. A new flower growing in the United States is the sanctuary and solidarity movement with the people of Central America and South Africa. In our global garden we need to cultivate the flower of justice for women wherever they live. There is no real justice until there is justice for women, and all the flowers of justice and humanity will grow when women stand together. They will grow in my country and in the revolutionary organization to which I belong. They will grow, and only then will all people be truly free to make the global garden their home.

My mother has given me so much, beautiful woman that she is. But now she has lost the little house and small pension that she and my father had accumulated after working their whole lives. She has lost it because of my work for human rights. She has been uprooted. That is what those of us who are refugees from lands suffering the pestilence of so-called civil strife and unrest are called: "uprooted people." According to all gardeners we should be dead by now.

Without roots, how can we survive? But hope and commitment to the struggle keep us alive. Many of us in Central America, and all oppressed and repressed communities of the world, are uprooted but miraculously still alive. That is one of the flowers in my mother's garden. That is her legacy to me. Like the grandmother spider in the Native American tradition, my mother and the mothers of our people bring out of their own substance the threads of life. They struggle but they never give up or surrender. The struggle is for always, one day at a time!

Mexico D.F.   Nov. 1987

Hermanas y hermanos de El Salvador
y del mundo entero,

En este capítulo comparto la he-
rencia que tengo de mi madre,
que es la misma que ella recibió:
Una tierra bella y fértil, por la
que hemos luchado, y continuare-
mos luchando hasta hacer
de ella la nueva Tierra de
la que habla Isaías - Dice que
los niños morirán de viejos, y
los viejos verán todos sus días.
Nadie se llevará sus cultivos,
ni nadie vivirá en sus vivien-
das más que ellos. Los pueblos
vivirán en Paz.

Hablo pues de nuestra lucha
y su relación con las otras
pueblos que también sufren
y se rebelan. Reflexiono también
sobre el significado de la soli-
daridad y el compañerismo, y
todo esto en el contexto de la
teología desde la mujer tercer-mun-
dista. Adelante mi pueblo,
Adelante Vamos!

8

From Garden to Table

Letty M. Russell

It is not easy to write about inheriting our mothers' gardens. I soon discovered this when I sat down to figure out how I could respond to the topic chosen for the 1987 Women's Interseminary Conference. The opportunity provided for doing feminist theology together in a global context has far outweighed the difficulties, but the ambiguity of the topic of our conversation, begun at Princeton Seminary in April 1987 and continued in this book, still remains.

I find it a difficult title because, even with the shift in emphasis from "search" to "inherit," I know that I cannot even approach the power of Alice Walker's article, "In Search of Our Mothers' Gardens."[1] In addition, I would much rather be *searching* than *inheriting.* I would rather be naming and claiming my own future together with my sisters. Instead, I find myself having to confess that as a white middle-class North American woman I have inherited benefits that accrue to me disproportionately because of the social structures of racism, classism, and imperialism. I also have to confess that a great deal of this results from my *fathers'* gardens and binds me to the patriarchal family structures out of which they have come.

Perhaps confession is good for more than the soul. It can be the means of remembering our inheritance, or lack thereof, and testing out, together with others, the ways that our parents' gardens may have been tended by the same hands and feet that trampled the gardens of Third World sisters and brothers, mothers and fathers. Such confession is truly difficult, but the sharing of garden stories may bear fruit for sharing around a global table where all are welcome. It may provide us with at least one way of picking up the agenda spelled out by Delores Williams in her article, "Women's Oppression and Lifeline Politics in Black Women's Religious Narratives." She speaks of the importance of relationships between women as a third aspect of women's experience, along with the experience of struggle and the experience of female body and culture. One of the tasks of feminist theology that she underlines is part of our agenda in this dialogue among white women and women of color.

Delores Williams urges us to work on mediating and healing the conflicts emerging as women of color and white women struggle together for empowerment, recognizing that white women must say no to traditional supportive alliances that are racist, and women of color must say no to forces of sexism in their community.[2] To do this we all need to take a critical look at our own inheritances. I will try to participate in this difficult task by describing my own mother's gardens.

Inheriting My Mother's Gardens

When I think back literally and symbolically to the gardens of my childhood, my first memory is of a victory garden. Some of you are not old enough to know what that was. A victory garden was not an early feminist plot to take over the home, not even one so deeply expressing the freedom and artistry of a mother like that of Alice Walker. Rather, it was full of things a child might not even want to eat, like swiss chard and beet greens, and it required a very definite expenditure of child labor in the weeding department. Victory gardens were planted almost everywhere, by almost everyone who could find some land, in order to help the war effort in World War II. Our garden was part of a fenced-in backyard behind a one-family house in the New Jersey suburb where I grew up. From the garden I could walk to the local Presbyterian church. I was so close, in fact, that I ran away from Sunday school in kindergarten, walked home, and announced to my surprised mother that it was boring!

I was very middle class, and the only time I came close to seeing the reality of the need to grow one's own food and save on everything, including money, was when my father's car business collapsed because of gas rationing and he was jobless for a year. My father had not been to college and had trouble finding a job he was willing to do. He had been rejected for military service because of a physical disability, although he had served in the navy during World War I.

The second garden of my childhood was that of the mysterious neighbors who lived on a hill behind our house on the other side of the block and owned a splendid garden that extended through several lots and contained a large goldfish pond. I was a tomboy and loved to go to this garden and its adjoining woods to pretend I was someone like Ayla in *Clan of the Cave Bear,* only in my day adventure stories were only about boys. I enjoyed playing so much that I paid little attention to school until the fourth grade, when I discovered adventure novels and finally learned to read.

The third garden of my childhood was a rather overgrown rose garden that grew by the sea toward the end of Long Island. This was my grandmother's garden, the grandmother Letty on my mother's side for whom I was named. Each summer I went to visit her and followed her around the hot, dusty garden, watering, cutting, and weeding, not because I had come to like gardening but because I loved her.

From my grandmother I learned to love the sea, and also the church that she served so extensively. Without a doubt she was my first conscious role model. I remember reading *A Tree Grows in Brooklyn,* trying to understand what it might have been like to grow up in Brooklyn. I wondered how it would feel to be valedictorian of my high school class and then go to work teaching piano lessons to support the family. All this was very difficult to imagine because my grandfather, an associate of John D. Rockefeller, was head of the legal division of Esso and had come from a brownstone mansion in Booklyn, not the tenement of the novel.

Rejecting My Mother's Gardens

Even with this mixed inheritance I had little trouble deciding which of the mothers' gardens to reject and which to accept as I graduated from Wellesley and entered the real world. Remembering my church and family connections, I did what every "normal" white middle-class woman did in 1951: I got married. I married a fellow leader in the Student Christian Movement who had graduated from Harvard and enrolled to study at Yale Divinity School. Thus in 1951 I found myself tending my first real parsonage garden in Higganum, Connecticut, where my husband was student pastor, and teaching third grade in Middletown to support his theological education. But there were no victory gardens there. The cats walked in the squash pies I baked for the church fair. I found myself substituting for my husband at church when he would suddenly take off, and the next thing I knew he had left me, my garden, *and* the church!

Somewhere in the process of losing my mother's primary garden, I decided, like many of you, that I did not have to have a vicarious ministry; I too could cultivate the life of a church community. And I found the opportunity to do so in East Harlem, in a not-so-vacant lot.

Although not a reality in my grandmother's life, the tenement with its occasional scruffy tree became the reality of my life for the next seventeen years. The only gardens in East Harlem had to be dug out of several feet of garbage and debris in a vacant lot as an annual church project. My community was not some romantic "clan of the cave bear" but ten thousand Black and Hispanic women, children, and men who struggled to sustain life in a city housing project where more than one third of the population was forced to live on welfare.

I ministered with a group of women and men who taught me about their own mothers' gardens and grew to reject much of my own parental gardens, yet to reclaim the power of God's liberating word for those who are struggling to be free. Bible study, preaching, and sacraments came alive as participation in freedom schools and civil rights demonstrations taught me firsthand what Mary's song about the mighty being cast down and the lowly being lifted up was all about (Luke 1:52).

Through my ministry as a Presbyterian pastor in the East Harlem Protestant Parish I was also drawn into national and international efforts to renew the church and build global partnership. Through the World Council of Churches, I met a Dutch ecumenist and missiologist named Hans Hoekendijk. Later, after studying with Hans when he came to teach World Christianity at Union Theological Seminary, I married this citizen of the world. Together we traveled and worked with people in many countries, so that I began to learn not only of my husband's Dutch and Indonesian mothers but also of the many women who were my partners around the world.

Walking in the Garden at Yale

Having left East Harlem to teach, I eventually found myself walking in the garden at Yale—a most dangerous place for me, and for many others as well. Sometimes when I try to support the use of inclusive language about God, or support affirmative action hiring, or am teaching liberation theology, I feel very much that I am more out of the garden than in it. Perhaps this is just as well, because this garden at Yale has a special danger for me: it is not so different from the parental gardens I fled. I feel a little like Lillith discovering that she really never escaped Adam's Eden after all!

As an elite professional I am cultivating many of my fathers' gardens, for it seems that they have been not only car dealers, jewelers, and businessmen but also New England whaling captains and pastors. My grandmother's grandmother was Letty Pierson, a granddaughter of Abraham Pierson, pastor in Clinton, Connecticut, and a founder of Yale.

As an uppity feminist woman I found that I still resembled my early role models: my grandmother and my mother, who recently celebrated her ninety-first birthday. I even inherited my ornery spirit from my Irish great-grandmother on my father's side. She was a pastor's widow who, having outlived two husbands, took her inheritance and founded a home for unwed mothers in Boston in the late 1800s. It seems that the Sweet Honey in the Rock singing group is right when their song, "We All, Every One of Us," declares that we have to come home again.[3]

Yale University is supported by corporate capitalism of a size my grandfather could never have dreamed, and so steeped in white male tradition that men of color and women of all colors find their mothers' pictures missing from the walls and their stories missing from history. It would seem that it might be harmful to their health and inheritance to do too much walking around that garden! Whether we share some of that inheritance, as I do, or whether we cannot even dimly recognize this old alma mater, those of us who walk in these gardens need to take steps to live as "betrayers of the betrayers" if we are to stay in such institutions.

My first clue to such subversive activity comes from long experience with being a *misfit*. If you are a tomboy and 5 feet 8 inches tall in the seventh grade, you never do fit female cultural norms. Most certainly a white middle-class woman never fits in a New York ghetto neighborhood, nor does she fit in a Christian Brothers men's college or (for that matter) in the ministry. Sometimes this being on the margin can give you the freedom to breathe, even freedom to maintain a self-critical stance toward the use of your own inheritance, if indeed this is a place where you find it worthwhile to continue the struggle.

My second clue to using my inheritance is *share it*. Whatever gifts God may have given us, we, like our mothers, are called to share those gifts in a solidarity of sisterhood that refuses to accept reality as it is. As Paula Giddings has put it, we need to learn from our Black mothers, who decided that the dream *was* the truth and then "would act and do accordingly." Like Martin Luther King, Jr., they had a dream . . . a dream more real than any "Real World 701."[4]

My last clue is that we need to cultivate the *inner resources* and wisdom necessary to living out these visions of full human community. I myself and the inheritance I carry with me can be dangerous to women of color. In order to come to supportive alliances and push ahead, I need to confront its oppressive aspects and live out the reality of a new household of freedom.[5] Delores Williams has reminded us that we may have to live like "rootless branches" if, as women of *all* colors, we separate ourselves from our racist, sexist, heterosexist, and classist past and create "a usable past" we can affirm together.[6]

Moving from Garden to Table

Recently, I tried to work on one way of moving out of our separate gardens toward a common table. With Katie Cannon I designed a course at Yale called Feminist Theology in Third World Perspective that would help participants own up to their divisions of sex, race, class, sexual orientation, language, and nationality as they joined in the search for global feminist theologies.[7] We sought to enter into this type of partnership for two reasons. One was the conviction that feminism is not truly advocacy for full human dignity of all women together with men if it is only white and Western. This conviction of many who call themselves feminist is underlined by Barbara Smith in an article on "Racism and Women's Studies." Feminism, she writes,

> is the political theory and practice that struggles to free *all* women: women of color, working-class women, poor women, disabled women, lesbians, old women—as well as white, economically privileged, heterosexual women. Anything less than this vision of total freedom is not feminism, but merely female self-aggrandizement.[8]

The other reason we wanted to move toward a global partnership in feminist theology was that we suspected this partnership needs to be worked out face-to-face in many groups and many places. It has been exciting to hear about the work of the Program on Theological Education and of the Sub-Unit on Women in Church and Society of the WCC in developing a Global Network of Women in Theological Education, and about the Women's Project of the Ecumenical Association of Third World Theologians. But we also wanted to share in the work by seeing what could be accomplished by teaching and learning together about how to move into global partnership. As Robin Morgan has pointed out in *Sisterhood Is Global,* an indigenous feminism has been present in every culture and period of history since the oppression of women began, and this tradition needs to be recovered and honored in the cultural context out of which it flowered.[9]

The class itself was not only taught with Katie Geneva Cannon, Associate Professor of Ethics at Episcopal Divinity School and Visiting Professor at Yale Divinity School. It was also planned and taught with five students of various racial backgrounds who served as teaching assistants and small-group leaders. The class was designed to help White, Afro-American, Hispanic, and Asian students move into dialogue with one another so they could discover the problems and resources of their own gardens and the possibilities for making the global connections.

Perspectives on Dialogue. There were three basic perspectives on how this dialogue might be facilitated, once persons had joined the class and thus made a commitment to struggle together against the usual exclusive hierarchical structures of university-based theological education in the United States. The first perspective was that women who are the underside of the underside were to be the ones with the hermeneutical or interpretive privilege. The questions, struggle, pain, and insight of those at the bottom were the basis of our learning together. Without this willingness to learn from those who are least powerful, the partnership dialogue cannot begin. Thus the course was taught with readings from African, Asian, and Latin-American women, and lectures and panels were presented by theologians such as Kwok Pui-lan, Mercy Oduyoye, and Ada María Isasi-Díaz, and by participants in the class.[10]

Second, the class was designed so that everyone could join in the dialogue because they shared in a "third thing" or task. The task was to learn about the social, political, economic, ecclesial structures that oppress women in all parts of the world and to work on what Katie Cannon calls "emancipatory historiography." That is, to work on how oppression has come about and on how to take steps together with others to work for change. For this reason time was spent not only on the stories and insights of women but also on analysis of their social, cultural, and historical context in relation to our own context in the center of U.S. neocolonialism, militarism, and multinational exploitation.

Last, the class was urged to work toward an understanding of global feminist theology by beginning in their own "mothers' gardens." By looking critically at their own racial, economic, and cultural history they could see how their theological understanding of God, themselves, and their neighbor shifted when they began to see the weeds and the flowers in their own garden in the light of those in other persons' home contexts. In this we were helped by the imagery of Alice Walker's *In Search of Our Mothers' Gardens,* as well as by the stories of the speakers and class panelists. Unless we dig deeply into our own garden and context, we have very little to share with others who want to join us at the global table.

Bringing Our Gifts to the Table. The commitment to move out of our gardens to the welcome table is a commitment to break down the barriers that separate us and to risk the transformation it will take for communities of partnership to survive in this oppressive world. But having made the commitment to struggle against oppression and for change, it is possible to bring whatever gifts we can find and move toward partnership at the global table. Perhaps three insights we discovered in our search for feminist theology in a Third World perspective will help us understand the process of moving toward partnership more clearly.

One insight we discovered was that moving toward a common table requires that we pay attention to what prevents people from coming to *"sit at the welcome table."*[11] Both personally and globally the road to freedom requires actions of imaginative and constructive repentance on the part of those whose history, culture, class, or actions have been responsible for the domination of others. Matthew 5:23–24 reminds us that it is not *we* who are to forgive our neighbor before we bring our gift to the altar; rather, our neighbor, who has something against *us,* has to forgive us. Reconciliation is not cheap; it does not begin with our asking for forgiveness, but rather with our taking action for change in solidarity with those who have been hurt. The poor do not ask us to feel guilty, for they can't eat guilt. What they ask is that we act to address the causes of injustice so they can obtain food.

In this interpretation of the "fencing of the table," those who are unbaptized or of a different denomination are welcome. And so are those who act in such a way that their neighbor can begin to trust them. For instance, as a white person working in a team ministry in East Harlem, New York, I found that I was accepted by my Black and Hispanic neighbors in spite of my white skin and clerical privilege, simply because I was at least trying to work for change in the community together with others. In the class, white women and

men were accepted by people of color when it was
clear that they were actually taking the risk of struggling for change in themselves and in the wider
society.

A second insight into ways of sharing our gifts in a
global community was a need to *discuss our theology
around the kitchen table.* That is, the theology that is
rooted among the oppressed of the oppressed does not
flourish in an academic context. Courses that begin
with ordinary stories of women as they gather around
their kitchen table or cooking area are not even
considered to be professional theology courses by
those who do so-called "classical" theology. Yet ap-
proaching the global table as partners requires that we
begin where people are and stay connected to the
reality of their lives. It is no accident that the press
that publishes writings by feminists of color in the
United States is called Kitchen Table: Women of
Color Press, or that when one man brought his
daughter to visit the class, she exclaimed to him,
"This is a different kind of class!"

In East Harlem apartments, almost everything happened around the kitchen table. People ate, cooked,
did homework, stacked groceries, and played cards,
all at the one available table. This is where we often
had house Bible study as well. In fact, the first paper I
wrote for the World Council of Churches was
developed out of a discussion of what salvation means
today in East Harlem.[12] After several cups of coffee
and much discussion, one woman said, "It means I'm
more free." Free to begin right there at the table to
work toward a global partnership that includes her
story.

The last insight we found about moving toward
partnership in global community was that we needed
to *create a round table.* We can't share together in our
struggle for justice if we do not make a place for all at
the welcome table. We have to make provision to

welcome all the gifts persons bring to the meal and design structures in community where there is no head or foot, no corners where persons get lost. In a wonderful poem entitled "In Search of a Round-table," Chuck Lathrop says that it will take some "sawing" to create this shape and thus may be painful.

> But the times and the tables
> Are changing and rearranging.[13]

A lot of things were rearranged in the class so that women of color could become the teachers of women and men of all colors, and so we could all gather around and talk with one another face-to-face as partners. In the East Harlem Protestant Parish we managed to do this by moving the communion table out of the chancel and giving it a very large round top that provided a comfortable center as we shared the word and sacrament together. In one Basic Christian Community in Nicaragua they did this by using the cross section of a large tree trunk as their altar.[14] In many places in Asia and Africa the welcome table is simply persons seated in a circle on the ground.

Of course, the point in all of this is not that we need one sort of table or even one set of gifts inherited from our gardens. What we do need is *one another!* We need one another's stories, pain, honesty, and laughter if we are to discern the power and the pain of our mothers' gardens in a way that bears fruit for the work of new creation.

NOTES

Introduction

1. The story of the theme selection was told to me by Susan Craig, one of the co-coordinators of the conference, at a New York meeting of the Ad Hoc Group on Racism, Sexism, and Classism (RSAC), October 24, 1987.

2. Alice Walker, *In Search of Our Mothers' Gardens* (San Diego, Calif.: Harcourt Brace Jovanovich, 1983), p. 241.

3. Mud Flower Collective, *God's Fierce Whimsy: Christian Feminism and Theological Education* (New York: Pilgrim Press, 1985).

4. Nellie Wong in Cherrie Moraga and Gloria Anzaldua, eds., *This Bridge Called My Back: Writings by Radical Women of Color* (Watertown, Mass.: Persephone Press, 1981), p. 178.

5. Derrick Bell, *And We Are Not Saved: The Elusive Quest for Justice* (New York: Basic Books, 1987); see Jeremiah 8:20.

Chapter 1
Mothers and Daughters, Writers and Fighters

These materials were presented at the Women's Interseminary Conference, Princeton, April 1987, and at a lecture series at Maryknoll entitled "Theological Voices of Third World Women,"

March 1987. The title is from the song written by Mary Sung-ok Lee that is quoted at the end of the chapter.

1. For an insightful discussion of the two different cultural systems, refer to Jacques Gernet, *China and the Christian Impact,* trans. Janet Lloyd (Cambridge: Cambridge University Press, 1985).

2. The Confucian tradition was criticized as patriarchal in the May Fourth Movement of 1919 and was more severely condemned in the Cultural Revolution during 1966–1976. In the post-Mao era, Chinese philosophers have begun to analyze the limits and contributions of the Confucian tradition as it relates to present Chinese society.

3. See for example, Mary Daly, *Beyond God the Father* (Boston: Beacon Press, 1973), and Rosemary Radford Ruether, *Sexism and God-Talk: Toward a Feminist Theology* (Boston: Beacon Press, 1983).

4. Ding Shujing, "Funü zai jiaohui de diwei" (Women's Status in the Church), *Nü Qing Nian* 7(2):22 (March 1928).

5. See Judith Plaskow, "Blaming Jews for Inventing Patriarchy," *Lilith* 7:12–13 (1980), and Elisabeth Schüssler Fiorenza, *In Memory of Her: A Feminist Theological Reconstruction of Christian Origins* (New York: Crossroad Publishing Co., 1983).

6. From Qu Yuan, "Li Sao" (Farewell Ode).

7. See "The History of Ms. Zhang Zhujun" in Li Youning and Zhang Yufa, eds., *Jindai Zhongguo nüquan yundong shiliao* (Historical Materials on Modern Chinese Feminist Movement), 2 vols. (Taibei: Biographical Literature Publisher, 1975), vol. 2, p. 1380.

8. Ruth Cheng, "Women and the Church," *Chinese Recorder* 53:540 (1922).

9. Carol P. Christ, "Spiritual Quest and Women's Experience," in Carol P. Christ and Judith Plaskow, eds., *Womanspirit Rising: A Feminist Reader in Religion* (San Francisco: Harper & Row, 1979), pp. 228–245. See also her *Laughter of Aphrodite: Reflections on a Journey to the Goddess* (San Francisco: Harper & Row, 1987).

10. See the poem of Alla Bozarth-Campbell, "Bakerwoman God," in Iben Gjerding and Katherine Kinnamon, eds., *No Longer Strangers: A Resource for Women and Worship* (Geneva: World Council of Churches, 1983), p. 54.

11. Gordon D. Kaufman, *The Theological Imagination: Constructing the Concept of God* (Philadelphia: Westminster Press, 1981), pp. 263–279.

12. John B. Cobb, Jr., "Feminism and Process Thought: A Two-way Relationship," in Sheila Greeve Davaney, ed., *Feminism and Process Thought* (Lewiston, N.Y.: Edwin Mellen Press, 1981), p. 42.

13. Used by permission of Mary Sung-ok Lee.

Chapter 2
Be a Woman, and Africa Will Be Strong

1. R. S. Rattray, *Ashanti Law and Constitution* (New York: Negro Universities Press, reprint 1969), pp. 270–284.

2. The Asenie group is one of seven divisions of the Asante people. All the divisions were founded by women. See Rattray, *Ashanti Law.*

3. My father (1905–1987), a Methodist educator and minister for all his working life, retired as Third President of Methodist Church Ghana (MCG). My mother lived *his* life.

4. The market days in West Africa follow patterns of four-, eight-, and sixteen-day periods.

5. *Christian Asor Ndwom* is the Fanti Methodist hymnbook of Methodist Church Ghana.

6. "The bringer of living water" is the title given to a newly born girl. The greeting goes as follows: *Abaayewa ma nsu* ("girl who gives water"), *waba a tema ase* ("now that you are here, stay with us").

Chapter 3
Following Naked Dancing and Long Dreaming

1. *Han* is the typical, most prevailing feeling of the Korean people. Korean theologian Hyun Young-Hak described our deep, shared feeling of *han* vividly: "Han is a sense of unresolved resentment against injustice suffered, a sense of helplessness because of the overwhelming odds against a feeling of total abandonment ("Why hast thou forsaken me?"), a feeling of acute pain, of sorrow in one's guts and bowels making the whole body writhe and wiggle, and an obstinate urge to take revenge and to right the wrong, all these combined." From Hyun Young-Hak's

unpublished lecture at James Memorial Chapel, Union Theological Seminary, New York, April 13, 1982, p. 7.

2. In Korean tradition, *ci-baji* women have been considered baby machines, giving birth to babies out of wedlock for privileged families. Most of them come from underprivileged political, economic, and social backgrounds. Although they take an active role in giving birth to a baby, they are considered little more than a body that produces a baby and do not have the right to keep their children.

3. The literal meaning of "yu-mo" is "milk-mother." These are women who breast-feed children who are not their own: wet nurses in English. These women come from underprivileged backgrounds too.

4. For the resource for women's life under Confucianism, see Lee Ock-Kyung, "A Study on Formational Condition and Settlement Mechanism of Jeong Juel (Faithfulness to Husband by Wife) Ideology of Yi Dynasty," M.A. thesis from Ewha Women's University, Seoul, Korea, 1985.

5. Fortune-tellers in Korea analyze people's destinies and tell their futures by looking at palm lines, face, etc. Their basic philosophy comes from a Korean-style mixture of Taoism, Shamanism, and Buddhism.

6. Ordained ministry has been a man's job in Korean Christian history. There are very few women ministers, and most of them are single. The majority of the denominations in Korea consider it illegal to ordain a married woman. Very few accept the ordination of married women.

7. Many Korean churches teach that drinking and smoking are serious sins. Korean society, as a whole, does not consider smoking and drinking acceptable behaviors for women.

8. Kwang-Ju was the site of many demonstrations against Japanese colonialism and dictatorship. It became a symbol of resistance in Korea, especially after the 1980 massacre, in which 2,000 civilians fighting for freedom and democracy were killed by the military.

9. Shamanism is a woman-centered popular religiosity in Korea. It has many gods but no creeds or dogmas or church buildings. Through shamanistic rituals, Koreans exorcise evil spirits, heal the sick, and console those who are oppressed.

10. In Korea, *tae-mong* plays an important role in determining the meaning of one's life. People believe that *tae-mong* is God's

prophecy for the baby. Most autobiographies or biographies begin with a description of the *tae-mong.* A baby is connected with all of the past and the future through *tae-mong.*

11. This impasse causes the feeling of *han* in oppressed people. For more information about the relationship between impasse and *han,* see Suh Nan-Dong, "Towards a Theology of Han," *Minjung Theology* (Singapore: Christian Council of Asia, 1981), pp. 51–69.

12. Alice Walker, *In Search of Our Mothers' Gardens* (San Diego, Calif.: Harcourt Brace Jovanovich, 1983), p.237.

13. *Minjung* means "grassroot people" in Korea. Minjung theology arose out of the Korean people's experience of suffering and liberation under the political dictatorship and economic exploitation of the 1970s.

14. My late mother's name.

15. My birth mother's name.

Chapter 4: Surviving the Blight

1. Sherley Anne Williams, Foreword to *Their Eyes Were Watching God,* by Zora Neale Hurston (Champaign, Ill.: University of Illinois Press, 1978), pp. vii–viii.

2. Victoria Byerly, *Hard Times Cotton Mill Girls: Personal Histories of Womanhood and Poverty in the South* (Ithaca, N.Y.: ILR Press, 1986), pp. 143–160.

3. Dorothy Sterling, ed., *We Are Your Sisters: Black Women in the Nineteenth Century* (New York: W. W. Norton & Co., 1984), pp. 42–43.

4. Ibid., p. 43.

5. George R. Rawick, *From Sundown to Sunup: The Making of the Black Community* (Westport, Conn.: Greenwood Publishing Co., 1972), p. 57.

6. Testimony of Sarah M. Grimké, abolitionist from South Carolina, in [Theodore D. Weld], *American Slavery As It Is: Testimony of a Thousand Witnesses* (American Anti-Slavery Society, 1839), cited in Gerda Lerner, ed., *Black Women in White America: A Documentary History* (New York: Vintage Books, 1972), p. 18.

7. Cited by Robert E. Hemenway in the Introduction to *Mules and Men,* by Zora Neale Hurston (Bloomington, Ind.: Indiana University Press, 1978), p. xxi.

8. Langston Hughes and Arna Bontemps, eds., *The Book of Negro Folklore* (New York: Dodd, Mead & Co., 1958), p. viii.

9. C. Eric Lincoln, *The Black Muslims in America* (Boston: Beacon Press, 1973), p. 35.

10. Rawick, p. 35.

11. Ibid.

Chapter 5: A Hispanic Garden in a Foreign Land

1. My understandings of culture are greatly influenced by Geertz and Scannone. See Clifford Geertz, *The Interpretations of Culture* (New York: Basic Books, 1973), and Juan Carlos Scannone, "Teología, Cultura Popular y Discernimiento," in *Cultura Popular y Filosofía de la Liberación* (Buenos Aires: Fernando Garcia Cambeiro, 1975), pp. 241–270.

2. As I type in my apartment I face a poster that reads, I AM A WOMAN GIVING BIRTH TO MYSELF.

3. *Building Feminist Theory: Essays from QUEST* (Harlow, Essex: Longman Group, 1981).

4. Marcia Ann Gillespie, "My Gloves Are Off, Sisters," *MS Magazine,* April 1987, pp. 19–20.

5. Ibid.

6. Three books that have been very important for me in the area of friendship are Margaret Farley, *Personal Commitments* (New York: Harper & Row, 1986); Isabel C. Heyward, *The Redemption of God* (Lanham, Md.: University Press of America, 1982); and Janice Raymond, *A Passion for Friends* (Boston: Beacon Press, 1986).

7. See Sonia Johnson, *Going Out of Our Minds: The Metaphysics of Liberation* (Freedom, Calif.: Crossing Press, 1987).

Chapter 6: From the Prairie to the World

1. Alice Walker, *In Search of Our Mothers' Gardens* (San Diego, Calif.: Harcourt Brace Jovanovich, 1983), p. 238.

2. Hendrik Kraemer, *The Theology of the Laity* (Philadelphia: Westminster Press, 1958).

3. See the Mud Flower Collective, *God's Fierce Whimsy: Christian Feminism and Theological Education* (New York: Pilgrim Press, 1985).

4. Joann Nash Eakin, "Toward a Global Network of Women in

Theological Education: The History of a Discovery and of a Vision; Some Proposed Possibilities," Program on Theological Education (Geneva: World Council of Churches, 1987), unpublished paper.

Chapter 8: From Garden to Table

1. Alice Walker, *In Search of Our Mothers' Gardens* (San Diego, Calif.: Harcourt Brace Jovanovich, 1983), pp. 231–243.

2. Delores Williams, "Women's Oppression and Lifeline Politics in Black Women's Religious Narratives," *Journal of Feminist Studies in Religion* 1(2):59–71 (Fall 1985).

3. Bernice Johnson Reagon, *Sweet Honey in the Rock: "We All . . . Every One of Us"* (Chicago: Song Talk Publishing Co., Flying Fish Records, 1983).

4. Paula Giddings, taped speech from the Riverside Church Convocation (New York: Riverside Church, October 8, 1986). Cf. Paula Giddings, *When and Where I Enter: The Impact of Black Women on Race and Sex in America* (New York: William Morrow & Co., 1984). For the powerful articulation of one woman's life, see Pauli Murray, *Song in a Weary Throat: An American Pilgrimage* (New York: Harper & Row, 1987).

5. See Letty M. Russell, *Household of Freedom: Authority in Feminist Theology* (Philadelphia: Westminster Press, 1987).

6. Williams, loc. cit., p. 71.

7. This course, whose title forms the subtitle of this book, was taught in the spring of 1987. It is also described in my article "Partnership in Models of Renewed Community," *Ecumenical Review* (in preparation).

8. Gloria T. Hull, Patricia Bell Scott, and Barbara Smith, eds., *All the Women Are White, All the Blacks Are Men, but Some of Us Are Brave: Black Women's Studies* (Old Westbury, N.Y.: Feminist Press, 1982), p. 49. Cf. Bell Hooks, *Feminist Theory from Margin to Center* (Boston: South End Press, 1984), p. 8.

9. Robin Morgan, ed., *Sisterhood Is Global: The International Women's Movement Anthology* (Garden City, N.Y.: Doubleday & Co., Anchor Books, 1984), p. 5.

10. See chapters 1, 2, and 5 in this book. See also John S. Pobee and Bärbel von Wartenberg-Potter, eds., *New Eyes for Reading: Biblical and Theological Reflections by Women from the Third World* (Geneva: World Council of Churches, 1986), and the Mud

Flower Collective, *God's Fierce Whimsy: Christian Feminism and Theological Education* (New York: Pilgrim Press, 1985), for written contributions by these women.

11. This spiritual, "Welcome Table," is quoted by Margaret Walker in her novel *Jubilee* (New York: Bantam Books, 1966), p. 58. I am indebted to Delores Williams for pointing out the use of welcome-table imagery in Afro-American religious tradition.

12. Letty M. Russell, "A Case Study from East Harlem," *Ecumenical Review,* July 1967, pp. 287–301.

13. *A Gentle Presence* (Washington, D.C., 1977), pp. 5–8. Quoted by Matthew Fox, *A Spirituality Named Compassion* (Minneapolis: Winston Press, 1979), p. 66.

14. Marguerite P. Bowes, "Report on a Trip to Nicaragua," oral report in the course Feminist Theology in Third World Perspective, Yale Divinity School, April 16, 1987.

ANNOTATED BIBLIOGRAPHY

Cecily P. Broderick y Guerra

African and Afro-American Women

Allison, Caroline. *"It's Like Holding the Key to Your Own Jail":
Women in Namibia.* Geneva: World Council of Churches, 1986.
  This brief history of women in Namibia offers information
which ordinary, uneducated, impoverished Namibian women
are forced to live with every day but which is unknown to
others.

Byerly, Victoria. *Hard Times Cotton Mill Girls: Personal Histories
of Womanhood and Poverty in the South.* Ithaca, N.Y.: ILR
Press, 1986.
  A history of work and life for Black and White women in the
mill towns of North Carolina, the book documents the obstacles
and tools for these women's survival.

Cannon, Katie Geneva. "Resources for a Constructive Ethic in the
Life and Work of Zora Neale Hurston." *Journal of Feminist
Studies in Religion* 1(1):37–51 (Spring 1985).
  This article is valuable on two counts: for its analysis of
the ethics evident in the writings and life of Hurston and
for its presentation of ethical study in the Black American
context.

———. "The Emergence of Black Feminist Consciousness." In

Feminist Interpretation of the Bible, ed. by Letty M. Russell. Philadelphia: Westminster Press, 1985. Pp. 30–40.

Cannon discusses the origin and definition of Black feminism, which, she claims, emerges out of and is a struggle which incorporates issues of gender, race, and class.

Christian, Barbara. *Black Feminist Criticism: Perspectives on Black Women Writers.* Elmsford, N.Y.: Pergamon Press, 1985.

A study of resources for Black feminist criticism drawing on writings by Black women—fictional, poetic, analytic, etc.—this essay offers an understanding of Black women's perspective of feminism and of Black women's literature.

Cliff, Michelle. "I Found God in Myself and I Loved Her Fiercely: More Thoughts on the Work of Black Women Artists." *Journal of Feminist Studies in Religion* 2(1):7–39 (Spring 1986).

When art by Africans and Afro-Americans (especially art by women) is used as a way to describe Afro-American women's theology, the art reveals that for Afro-American or Black women their private relationship with God takes precedence over all other relationships.

Giddings, Paula. *When and Where I Enter: The Impact of Black Women on Race and Sex in America.* New York: William Morrow & Co., 1984.

A history of racism and sexism in the enfranchisement (read Black male enfranchisement) and suffrage (read White women's suffrage) movements in America. The contributions of Black women are recorded, along with betrayals by White women and the ambivalence of Black men. Includes a bibliography.

Gilkes, Cheryl Townsend. "The Roles of Church and Community Mothers: Ambivalent American Sexism or Fragmented African Familyhood?" *Journal of Feminist Studies in Religion* 2(1):41–59 (Spring 1986).

Both secular and ecclesiastical organizations within the Black community rely upon the leadership of Black women (mother figures). Gilkes discusses the factors that define the work of these women.

Hooks, Bell. *Ain't I a Woman? Black Women and Feminism.* Boston: South End Press, 1981.

Hooks examines the impact of sexism and racism on Black women from the period of slavery to the present day and concludes with suggestions for the future of a feminist theory that takes this fuller view of history into account. Includes a bibliography.

————. *Feminist Theory from Margin to Center.* Boston: South End Press, 1984.

Primarily a critique of feminist theory, this book takes on the task defined in *Ain't I a Woman?* by presenting a feminist theory that takes not just sexism into account but also racism, classism, and heterosexism. Feminism, according to the author, should be the struggle to eradicate all ideologies of domination. Includes a bibliography.

Jordan, June. *On Call: Political Essays.* Boston: South End Press, 1985.

A collection of political essays for the continuing education of global or national activists.

Joseph, Gloria, and Jill Lewis. *Common Differences: Conflicts in Black and White Feminist Perspectives.* Garden City, N.Y.: Doubleday & Co., Anchor Books, 1981.

Analyzes the schisms between Black and White women in the women's movement, using interviews of a diverse group of Black and White women: rich, poor, and middle-class; educated and illiterate; lesbian and heterosexual; radical and conservative. An important book for women struggling to work with and relate to other women across racial lines.

Lorde, Audre. *Sister Outsider: Essays and Speeches.* Freedom, Calif.: Crossing Press, 1984.

A Black, lesbian, feminist mother on the cutting edge of feminist consciousness deals with a variety of topics such as anger, finding tools to dismantle patriarchal and racially supremist societies, and the importance of poetry (i.e., the writing form of racial-ethnic women) for the formation of political consciousness and action.

Mandela, Winnie. *A Part of My Soul Went with Him.* Ed. by Anne Benjamin and Mary Benson. New York: W. W. Norton & Co., 1984.

This personal chronicle of Mandela's own oppression and commitment to freedom makes real and immediate the need to end apartheid in South Africa. The author discusses what being a political leader is like and what it is to be married to a political leader.

Noble, Jeanne. *Beautiful, Also, Are the Souls of My Black Sisters: A*

History of the Black Woman in America. Englewood Cliffs, N.J.: Prentice-Hall, 1978.

An examination of the lives and work of leading Black American women, this book gives not only facts but also a perspective omitted from American and Black American history texts.

Oduyoye, Mercy Amba. *And Women: Where Do They Come In?* Methodist Church Nigeria (Woodfree Community Enterprises, Private Mail Bag 1041, Mushin, Logos State, Nigeria).

A discussion by a Ghanaian woman of the sacramental ordination of women and an argument for the elimination of discrimination against women in the church.

―――. *Hearing and Knowing: Theological Reflections on Christianity in Africa.* Maryknoll, N.Y.: Orbis Books, 1986.

The first part of this book presents theology in Africa; past and present; the second presents themes in African theology. According to the author, Christianity's positive role in Africa will be determined by its respect for and use of Africa's resources.

―――. "Reflection from a Third World Woman's Perspective: Women's Experience and Liberation Theologies." In *Irruption of the Third World: Challenge to Theology,* ed. by Virginia Fabella and Sergio Torres. Maryknoll, N.Y.: Orbis Books, 1981.

The author develops a Third World feminist theology.

―――, ed. *The State of Christian Theology in Nigeria 1980–1981.* Ibadan, Nigeria: Daystar Press, 1986.

A collection of essays on the challenges of Nigerian society to Christian theology and the challenges of Christianity to Nigeria. Topics include: Mariology, living within multicultural communities, and prayer in indigenous churches.

Steady, Filomina Chioma, ed. *The Black Woman Cross-Culturally.* Cambridge, Mass.: Schenkman Books, 1985.

A diverse collection of essays on Black women's position in traditional, historical, and contemporary societies, divided into four parts: Africa, the United States, South America, and the Caribbean.

Thiam, Awa. *Black Sisters, Speak Out: Feminism and Oppression in Black Africa.* Tr. by Dorothy Blair. London: Pluto Press, 1986.

Black African women speak for themselves about their

oppression. Particular attention is paid to male control and mutilation of women's bodies through social norms and religious institutions.

Walker, Alice. *The Color Purple.* San Diego, Calif.: Harcourt Brace Jovanovich, 1982.

As it presents a picture of farming and family life among Black Americans, this novel offers a view of Black women's theology and ethics as manifested in the everyday lives of Black women.

———. *In Search of Our Mothers' Gardens.* San Diego, Calif.: Harcourt Brace Jovanovich, 1983.

What is a Black feminist? A womanist? These essays explore the nature of womanist life, thought, and work.

Walker, Margaret. *Jubilee.* New York: Bantam Books, 1966.

Jubilee traces the life of a Black woman through slavery, the Civil War, and Reconstruction. It contains truth *Gone with the Wind* omits.

Williams, Delores. "Women's Oppression and Lifeline Politics in Black Women's Religious Narratives." *Journal of Feminist Studies in Religion* 1(2):59–71 (Fall 1985).

A study of the relationship of religion, politics, and everyday life—"lifeline politics"—using fiction by Black women as the resource.

Zoe-Obianga, Rose. "Resources in the Tradition for the Renewal of Community." *Women: Third World Theology* 8(3):73–77 (September 1985).

African tradition, Zoe-Obianga claims, is the primary and critical source for reshaping African Christianity pervaded by patriarchal and Western ideologies.

Asian and Asian-American Women

An Ocean with Many Shores: Asian Women Making Connections in Theology and Ministry. A Report of the National Conference of Asian Women Theologians (Northeast U.S. Group), June 6–9, 1986 (AWT Program Coordinator, P.O. Box 374, Warwick, NY 10990-0374).

This booklet is a resource for further reading about this group as well as a report on the June conference. The final section is a bibliography.

Brock, Rita Nakashima. "Special Section: Asian Women Theologians Respond to American Feminism." *Journal of Feminist Studies in Religion* 3(2):103–105 (Fall 1987).

This article is an introduction to the section of papers presented by the Asian Women Theologians network before the Women and Religion Section of the American Academy of Religion. The section also includes papers by Patria Agustín, Yasuko Morihara Grosjean, Kwok Pui-lan, and Soon-Hwa-Sun.

Cho, Wha Soon. *Let the Weak Be Strong: A Woman's Struggle for Justice.* Oak Park, Ill.: Meyer Stone Books, 1988.

Edited by Lee (Park) Sun Ai and Ahn Sang Nim, this is a firsthand account of Reverend Cho's ministry with the women industrial workers in Korea.

Fabella, Virginia. "Overview of Ecumenical Association of Third World Theologians (EATWOT) in Asia." *Voices from the Third World* 7(2):7–13 (December 1984).

This was the opening address at the sixth conference of EATWOT. It discusses the reformulation of Christian theology in Asia and proposes the utilization of the peoples, cultures, and religious traditions of Asia as resources.

Gallup, Padma. "Doing Theology—An Asian Feminist Perspective." *Bulletin of the Commission on Theological Concerns, Christian Conference of Asia* 4(3):21–27 (December 1983).

Explores a New Asian theology, Asian Imago Dei, using Hindu symbolism, Indian women's issues, and feminist theology.

Gnanadason, Aruna. "Human Rights and Women's Concerns." *Religion and Society* 28(1):15(1981).

The executive secretary of the All Indian Council of Christian Women talks about women's concerns.

Katoppo, Marianne. *Compassionate and Free: An Asian Woman's Theology.* Maryknoll, N.Y.: Orbis Books, 1979.

Woman as the Other, woman's liberation, and women in Asian theology are discussed from the Indonesian perspective.

Kingston, Maxine Hong. *The Woman Warrior.* New York: Alfred A. Knopf, 1976.

The memoirs of a Chinese woman immigrant in the United States. The author talks about how the legends of the woman warrior she heard in childhood affect her self-image and explores the conflicts and benefits of Asian-American women's multicultural life.

Korean Association of Women Theologians (KAWT). "Consultation Toward the Establishing of Asian Feminist Theology—A Report." *Bulletin of the Commission on Theological Concerns, Christian Conference of Asia* 4(3):34–38 (December 1983).

Examines the nature of Korean feminist theology and establishes the following agenda: Interpret scripture from a feminist viewpoint; democratize the church; reinterpret Korean culture in line with feminist theology; address problems of a divided country and work for reunification; and establish cooperation between Asian churchwomen.

Kwok, Pui-lan. "God Weeps with Our Pain." *East Asian Journal of Theology* 2(2):228–232 (1984).

Feminist theology using poems, lullabies, and stories from Asia.

———. "The Feminist Hermeneutics of Elisabeth Schüssler Fiorenza: An Asian Feminist Response." *East Asian Journal of Theology* 3(2):147–153 (1985).

A critical study of Schüssler Fiorenza's hermeneutics, discussing how useful it is in the Asian context.

Lee, Inn Sook, ed. *Korean-American Women: Toward Self-Realization.* Association of Korean Christian Scholars in North America, 490 Davey Avenue, Mansfield, Ohio, 1985.

Essays to support and encourage Korean-American women and other racial-ethnic women seeking freedom from cultural and societal oppression. Includes a bibliography.

Lee, Sun-ai, and Don Luce, eds. *The Wish: Poems of Contemporary Korea.* New York: Friendship Press, 1983.

Poems written by Korean farmers, workers—children, women, and men—in Korean and English, illustrated with Korean drawings; the poems are about the hopes, fears, dreams, and struggles of the people.

Lee, Sung-Hee. "Women's Liberation Theology as the Foundation for Asian Theology." *East Asian Journal of Theology* 4(2):2–13 (1986).

Uses images of Korean women in literature and their place in society to understand the contributions the Korean women's movement and women's liberation theology make to Asian theology.

Lewis, Nantawan Boonprasat. "Asian Women's Theology: A Historical and Theological Analysis." *East Asian Journal of Theology* 4(2):18–22 (1986).

This essay considers the use of scripture, the concept of Godhead, Christology, and the place of other cultural and religious traditions in Asian feminist theology.

Mananzan, Mary John, ed. *Essays on Women.* Saint Scholastica's College, 2560 Leon Guinto Street, P.O. Box 3153, Manila, Philippines, 1987.

This is the first anthology of essays by Philippine women after the February Incident of 1986, reflecting on the status of women, gender politics, and women's movements in the Philippines.

Matsui, Yayori, and Sun-ai Park. "Theological Reflection on Prostitution Industry." *Bulletin of the Commission on Theological Concerns, Christian Conference of Asia* 4(3):2–10 (December 1983).

A journalist for a leading Japanese daily newspaper and the editor of *In God's Image* discuss the Asian prostitution industry.

Niguidula, Lydia N. "Women in Theology Revolutionizing Liturgy." *Bulletin of the Commission on Theological Concerns, Christian Conference of Asia* 4(3):32–33 (December 1983).

An Asian theology of liturgy, celebrating life in the midst of pain and danger and insecurity.

Park, Sun-ai. "Asian Women's Role in Church and Society." *Midstream* 25(1):57–64 (January 1986).

Women's roles in Hinduism, Buddhism, Taoism, and Islam are considered in order to understand roles Asian women currently have and may take in Christianity.

———. "Asian Women's Theological Reflection." *East Asian Journal of Theology* 3(1):172–182 (Spring 1987).

A discussion of Asian women's theology; its relevancy, truthfulness to the Judeo-Christian tradition, and connection to liberation theology are considered.

———. "The Women's Movement and Ecumenical Agenda." *In God's Image,* April 1985, pp. 40–46.

This paper deals with three topics: women in the divided world, the women's movement as a renewal force, and women's power for unity.

Reading the Bible as Asian Women. Women's Concerns Unit, Christian Conference of Asia, 1986.

This book is a collection of Bible studies and reflections on the themes of poverty, justice, and freedom by women from ten Asian countries.

Southard, Naomi, and Rita Nakashima Brock. "The Other Half of the Basket: Asian American Women and the Search for a Theological Home." *Journal of Feminist Studies in Religion* 3(2):135–150 (Fall 1987).

Asian-American women speak for themselves in interviews with sixteen of the sixty-six known Asian-American women in ministry. The article addresses four areas of concern to Asian-American women: their multicultural context, the community of creation, creating a ministry of relationship, and the need for healing. It concludes with a summary of the differences between and growth points for Asian-American and White American feminist theologies.

"Suggested Readings on Asian Women and Theology." *In God's Image,* April 1986, pp. 47–51. An annotated bibliography of material written by Asian women and about issues (e.g., theological, political, social) concerning Asian women in Burma, China, India, Indonesia, Japan, Korea, Malaysia, the Philippines, Thailand, and America.

Latin-American/Hispanic Women

Amancida Collective. *Revolutionary Forgiveness: Feminist Reflections on Nicaragua.* Maryknoll, N.Y.: Orbis Books, 1987.

Thirteen North Americans share what they learned about U.S. involvement in Nicaragua and about the faith and life of Nicaraguans from the people of Nicaragua. The working process for this collective is similar to that used by the Mud Flower Collective.

Bandarage, Asoka. "Reflections from Texas: Spirituality, Community, and Women of Color." *Women of Power* 4:38–40 (Fall 1986).

Women of color (in particular Marta Benavides, a contributor to this book) speak for themselves about their lives, careers, and commitment to justice.

Cabral, Sara. "Women in Struggle." *Lucha: Struggle* 8(4):14–19 (September 1984).

An overview of the contributions Latin-American women have made to the struggles for justice and freedom in their countries.

Camacho de Schmidt, Aurora. "A Message from a Hispanic Woman to Woman Church Gathered in Chicago." *American Friends Service Committee,* 1501 Cherry Street, Philadelphia, PA 19102.

A Latin-American woman assumes her place (*tierra*) wherein she is assumed to be out of place (*destierro*).

Carlessi, Carolina. "Latin American Women Confront Patriarchy." *Latinamerica Press,* August 25, 1983, p. 1.

A report on the Second Feminist Encounter for Latin America and the Caribbean. The meeting focused on the need to establish feminism so it can contribute to the whole fabric of society.

Chanduvf, Elsa. "No More 'Chancletas': The Language and Practice of Machismo." *Latinamerica Press,* May 31, 1984, p. 6.

The article analyzes the forms and functions of machismo—sexism—in the church and in cultural and family structures of Latin America.

Cuadra, Ludmila. "Andean Labor Calls for Unity." *Latinamerica Press,* August 25, 1983, pp. 1–8.

A report on the meeting of the first general session of the Andean Labor Council. Central themes considered: patriarchy in its relation to daily life, salaried work, health, violence, sexuality, history. Racism and lesbianism also were considered.

Ferro, Cora. "The Latin American Woman: The Praxis and Theology of Liberation." *The Challenge of Basic Christian Communities,* ed. by Sergio Torres and John Eagleson. Maryknoll, N.Y.: Orbis Books, 1981.

Ferro reports on a meeting of women from all over Latin America involved with grassroots movements, at which they reflected on the issues and problems confronting women. The article concludes with concrete suggestions to end oppression and rebuild communities of liberation.

Isasi-Díaz, Ada María, "Toward an Understanding: Feminismo Hispano in U.S.A." In *Women's Consciousness: Women's Conscience,* ed. by Barbara H. Andolsen, Christine E. Gudorf, and Mary D. Pellaver. San Francisco: Winston Press, 1985.

A look at feminist Hispanics in the United States and horizontal violence (Hispanic/Black; Hispanic/White; Hispanic feminist/Hispanic men).

————and Yolanda Tarango. *Hispanic Women: Prophetic Voice in the Church.* New York: Harper & Row, 1988.

This text develops a Hispanic woman's liberation theology and religious practices.

Ress, Mary Judith. "Feminist Theologians Challenge Churches on Patriarchal Structures." *Latinamerica Press,* May 21, 1984, pp. 3–4.

Latin-American feminist theologians discuss sexism. They see sexism within, not apart from, the overall situation of oppression suffered by the continent's poor.

Tamez, Elsa. *The Bible of the Oppressed.* Tr. by J. O'Connell. Maryknoll, N.Y.: Orbis Books, 1982.

Biblical analysis from the perspective of those oppressed by poverty and sexism. The author is a Costa Rican, a woman, and a biblical scholar.

————. "Women and the Bible," *Lucha: Struggle* 9(3):54–64 (June 1985).

This article offers a new hermeneutical criteria (feminist and Third World) and applies it to the circumstances of Latin-American women.

————. *Against Machismo: Rubem Alves, Leonardo Boff, Gustavo Gutiérrez, José Míguez Bonino, Juan Luis Segundo and Others Talk About the Struggle of Women.* Oak Park, Ill.: Meyer-Stone Books, 1987.

A book that draws male Latin-American liberation theologians into dialogue around issues of women's oppression in the church and society.

Tarango, Yolanda. "At the Most Basic Level." *The Church Woman,* Spring 1986, pp. 33–37.

Tarango speaks of her work and the women who come to Visitation House, a home where women reach out to women.

Trapasso, Rosa Dominga. "The Feminization of Poverty." *Latinamerica Press,* May 31, 1984, p. 5.

An analysis of the feminization of poverty from data and firsthand experience.

"Women's Lives in El Salvador." *ISIS International* 19 (1981).

This issue documents the struggle for life and future among the women of El Salvador.

White American Women and the Third World

Collins, Sheila. "The Economic Basis of Racism and Sexism." *Theology in the Americas.* Documentation Series No. 13, November 1980.

This paper explores the interdependence of racism, sexism, and capitalism.

―――. "Religion, Class, and Ethnicity in Coalition Politics." *Churches in Struggle,* ed. by William K. Tabb. New York: Monthly Review Press, 1986.

A discussion of the strategies the 1984 Jesse Jackson presidential campaign offers to progressive movements.

Harrison, Beverley, *Making the Connections: Essays in Feminist Social Ethics,* ed. by Carol Robb. Boston: Beacon Press, 1985.

This collection makes the connection between social reality and the way we act and think.

Heyward, Carter. "Heterosexist Theology: Being Above It All." *Journal of Feminist Studies in Religion* 3(1):29–38 (Spring 1987).

An analysis of liberal theology and its affirmation of heterosexism.

―――. "An Unfinished Symphony of Liberation: The Radicalization of Christian Feminism Among U.S. White Women." *Journal of Feminist Studies in Religion* 1(1):99–118 (Spring 1985).

Discusses recent contributions to Christian feminism.

Moltmann, Jürgen, and M. Douglas Meeks. "Liberation of Oppressors." *Christianity and Crisis* 38(20):310–317.

Oppression destroys humanity on two fronts: through evil and through suffering. This article provides a theology and praxis for people dehumanized by evil oppressors. It is one of the few writings about liberation theology that addresses the question: What do liberation theologies have to say to oppressors?

Rich, Adrienne. "Resisting Amnesia: History and Personal Life." *MS Magazine,* March 1987, pp. 66–67.

Rich explores the significance of history, in particular Black

History Month (February) and Women's History Month (March), to feminists.

Russell, Letty, ed. *Changing Contexts of Our Faith.* Philadelphia: Fortress Press, 1985.

A collection of essays on nurturing faith through change. Can be used as a study guide for Christians committed to justice in their faith and work.

―――. *Household of Freedom: Authority in Feminist Theology.* Philadelphia: Westminster Press, 1987.

This book addresses the question of what legitimate power is in the context of Christianity. It is important reading for people in positions of authority and for people coping with the authority of others.

Stallard, Karin, et al. *Poverty in the American Dream: Women and Children First.* Boston: South End Press, 1983.

An educational tool, this booklet teaches about the reality of poverty: its feminization and abuse of children.

Smith, Lillian. *Killers of the Dream.* New York: W.W. Norton & Co., 1949.

The personal narrative of a White North American woman's effort to understand and then reject her own racism.

Global Resources

Allen, Paula Gunn. *The Sacred Hoop: Recovering the Feminine in American Indian Traditions.* Boston: Beacon Press, 1986.

Allen explores Indian female deities, American Indian women's history, the honored place of lesbians in Indian culture, and the importance of mothers and grandmothers to the Indian identity. Includes a bibliography.

Bataille, Gretchen M., and Kathleen Mullen Sands. *American Indian Women: Telling Their Lives.* Lincoln, Nebr.: University of Nebraska Press, 1984.

A collection of autobiographies by American Indian women. Gives firsthand information about these women's lives, culture, and relation to White America. Includes a bibliography.

Cameron, Anne. *Daughters of Copper Woman.* Vancouver, B.C.: Press Gang Publishers, 1981.

At their request, the author shares stories told her by the native people of Vancouver Island.

Eck, Diana L., and Devaki Jain, eds. *Speaking of Faith: Global Perspectives on Women, Religion, and Social Change.* Philadelphia: New Society, 1987.

Essays by twenty-six women from five continents representing major world religions, searching for a common religious foundation for social justice.

Fabella, Virginia, and Mercy Amba Oduyoye, eds. *Third World Women Doing Theology.* Maryknoll, N.Y.: Orbis Books, 1988.

Papers from the First International Women's Conference of the Ecumenical Association of Third World Theologians, December 1–6, 1986, Oaxtepec, Mexico.

Fabella, Virginia, and Sergio Torres, eds. *Doing Theology in a Divided World.* Maryknoll, N.Y.: Orbis Books, 1985.

The product of the Sixth Conference of the Ecumenical Association of Third World Theologians (EATWOT). The conference consisted of a dialogue between First and Third World theologians. Includes an essay by Mercy Amba Oduyoye.

Fuentes, Annette, and Barbara Ehrenreich. *Women in the Global Factory.* Boston: South End Press, 1984.

This booklet presents the problems of women working in factories and considers ways to deal with "free zones," child labor, and the search for cheap labor markets in Third World nations with troubled economies.

Gonzalez, Justo and Catherine. *In Accord: Let Us Worship.* New York: Friendship Press, 1981.

A globally inclusive liturgical resource book written from a liberation theology perspective.

Haddad, Yvonne Yazbeck, and Ellison Banks Findly, eds. *Women, Religion, and Social Change.* Albany, N.Y.: State University of New York Press, 1985.

This book explores the relationship between women and traditional religious systems: Judaic, Christian, Buddhist, Hindu, Islamic, North American Indian, etc.

Moraga, Cherrie, and Gloria Anzaldua, eds. *This Bridge Called My Back: Writings by Radical Women of Color.* Watertown; Mass.: Persephone Press, 1981.

Anthology of writings (poems, stories, autobiographical essays) by racial-ethnic women. This text gives firsthand accounts of lesbian and heterosexual, Hispanic, Asian, Black, etc., women's suffering and survival.

Global Resources   179

Morgan, Robin, ed. *Sisterhood Is Global: The International Women's Movement Anthology.* Garden City, N.Y.: Doubleday & Co., Anchor Books, 1984.

Articles by feminists throughout the world preceded by statistics on the status of women in each country considered.

Mud Flower Collective. *God's Fierce Whimsy: Christian Feminism and Theological Education.* New York: Pilgrim Press, 1985.

The Mud Flower Collective is a group of women in theological higher education. *God's Fierce Whimsy* is the product of their discussion, study, work, prayer, commitment, and reflection. It is valuable not only for the topics considered—the content, method, and obstacles to seminary education—but as an example for people (such as the contributors to this book) working in partnership for justice in religious institutions and society at large. Includes bibliography.

Parvey, Constance F., ed. *The Community of Women and Men in the Church: The Sheffield Report.* Geneva: World Council of Churches, 1983.

This book reports on a four-year international and ecumenical study of men and women in the church. The manner in which the issues (regarding theology, participation, and relationship of women and men in the church) are presented invites the reader's own questions and reflections.

Pobee, John S., and Bärbel von Wartenberg-Potter, eds. *New Eyes for Reading: Biblical and Theological Reflections by Women from the Third World.* Geneva: World Council of Churches, 1986.

Essays and reflections by women from Africa, Asia, and Latin America on the Bible, church, and society. The articles are both critical of traditional understandings and creative, suggesting ways for indigenous reappropriation of tradition.

Ross, Paula, ed. *My Story's On! Ordinary Women, Extraordinary Lives.* Berkeley, Calif.: Common Differences Press, 1985.

Women of the "wrong" color, gender, class, or sexuality claim their place in the world and, in the process, make the world more just by telling their own stories.

Wartenberg-Potter, Bärbel von, ed. *By Our Lives: Stories of Women, Today and in the Bible.* Geneva: World Council of Churches, 1985.

A collection of stories and reflections about women today and in the Bible which reveals the role and authority of the Bible for Third World women.

Webster, John C. B., and Ellen Low Webster, eds. *The Church and Women in the Third World.* Philadelphia: Westminster Press, 1985.

Women and men, Protestants and Catholics, First and Third World writers present the results of empirical research on Christian images of women, the role of women in the church, and the impact the church has on the status of women.

Periodicals Related to Third World Feminist Theology

Africa World Press, P.O. Box 1892, Trenton, NJ 08607

Bulletin of the Commission on Theological Concerns, Christian Conference of Asia, 480 Lorong 2 Tao Payoh, Singapore 1231

Central America Resource Center, P.O. Box 2327, Austin, TX 78768

East Asian Journal of Theology, 4 Mount Sophia, Singapore 0922, Republic of Singapore

El Rostro Femenino de la Teología (a Spanish-language publication), Editorial Departamento Ecuménico de Investigaciones, Apartido 390-2070, Sabanilla, San Jose, Costa Rica

D.E.I., Departamento Ecuménico de Investigaciones, Apartido 390-2070, Sabanilla, San Jose, Costa Rica

In God's Image, Christian Conference of Asia, 10 New Industrial Road, Singapore 1953

Lucha: Struggle, New York Circus: Center for Social Justice and International Awareness, P.O. Box 37, Times Square Station, New York, NY 10108

Noticias (the Spanish-language publication) or *Latinamerica Press* (the English-language publication), Apartado 6694, Lima 100, Peru

Journal of Feminist Studies in Religion, Membership Services, P.O. Box 1608, Decatur, GA 30031–1608

Voices from the Third World, Center for Society and Religion, 281 Deans Road, Colombo 10, Sri Lanka

Women of Power, P.O. Box 827, Cambridge, MA 00238

Women in a Changing World, World Council of Churches, 150 route de Ferney, 1211 Geneva 20, Switzerland

Women in Action, 1S1S International, Via Santa Maria dell'
Anima 30, 00186, Rome, Italy

Women's International Resource Exchange (WIRE), 2700 Broad-
way, Room 7, New York, NY 10025

Women's Review of Books, Wellesley College Center for Research
on Women, Wellesley, MA 02181